Barbara
Hanseman

D1350502

A Student's Guide to
The Selected Poems of T. S. Eliot

A STUDENT'S GUIDE
TO
THE SELECTED POEMS
OF
T. S. ELIOT

B. C. Southam

FABER AND FABER
3 Queen Square
London

First published in 1968
by Faber and Faber Limited
3 Queen Square London WC1
Reprinted 1969, 1971 and 1972
Printed in Great Britain by
Latimer Trend & Co Ltd Plymouth
All rights reserved

ISBN 0 571 09277 2 (Faber Paper Covered Edition)

Contents

CONTENTS

THE HOLLOW MEN

ASH-WEDNESDAY

APPENDIX
The Composition of *The Waste Land*,
The Hollow Men and *Ash-Wednesday*

Acknowledgments

I would like, first, to thank Mrs. T. S. Eliot for her interest and advice in the preparation of this book. I am most grateful for the suggestions and corrections which she has so kindly and patiently advanced. My second, and more general debt, is to the long line of scholars and critics who have written on the poetry of Eliot. I have drawn upon hundreds of books and articles, and consulted thousands of notes, so many that a full list of acknowledgments would be pages long. At the risk of discourtesy, I would like to excuse myself from such a listing, mentioning instead only the key-works, from which I have learnt much in my general approach to Eliot and in the treatment of specific details. These works are listed below; and of these I must acknowledge my prime debt to the one indispensable guide to Eliot's sources and references—*T. S. Eliot's Poetry and Plays* by Professor Grover Smith.

Finally, I am grateful for this opportunity to express my thanks to a number of colleagues and friends who have been kind enough to let me make use of their judgement and scholarship: Miss Lesley Brown of Routledge & Kegan Paul; F. W. Bateson, Corpus Christi College, Oxford; Martin Dodsworth, University of London; Professor J. C. Maxwell, Balliol College, Oxford; Hyam Maccoby, Dr. Roger Gard, Canon Frank Colquhoun; Antony Woolf, who helped me in fact-finding; and Stephen Erskine-Hill, whose discussions with me of the *Selected Poems* called this book into being. But, inevitably, despite all advice and correction, there will be errors of fact and omission, and notes which will seem fanciful, wrongheaded or eccentric. These imperfections are my responsibility.

SELECT BIBLIOGRAPHY

Brooks, Cleanth, *Modern Poetry and the Tradition*, London 1948, New York 1965.

Drew, Elizabeth, *T. S. Eliot, the Design of his Poetry*, New York 1949, London 1950.

Frye, Northrop, *T. S. Eliot*, London 1963, New York 1966.

Gardner, Helen, *The Art of T. S. Eliot*, London 1949, New York 1959.

Howarth, Herbert, *Notes on Some Figures Behind T. S. Eliot*, New York 1964, London 1965.

Kenner, Hugh, *The Invisible Poet: T. S. Eliot*, New York 1959.

Matthiessen, F. O., and Barber, C. L., *The Achievement of T. S. Eliot: an essay on the nature of poetry* (1935), enlarged edition London and New York 1958.

Smith, Grover, *T. S. Eliot's Poetry and Plays: a study in source and meaning*, Chicago 1956, revised edition 1960.

Unger, Leonard, *T. S. Eliot: Movements and Patterns*, London and Minneapolis, 1966.

Williamson, George, *A Reader's Guide to T. S. Eliot: a poem-by-poem analysis*, London and New York, revised edition 1955.

Note on Revised Edition

In this revised edition, the opportunity has been taken to correct errors and add some further notes, the most important of these arising from the discovery in 1968 of a collection of Eliot's manuscripts. Amongst these papers (described by Donald Gallup in the *Times Literary Supplement*, 7th November 1968, and in the *Bulletin of the New York Public Library*, vol. 72, December 1968) is the manuscript of *The Waste Land*, drafts of nearly thirty hitherto unpublished poems and fragments, and manuscripts of a number of the early *Selected Poems* (including 'Preludes', 'The Love Song of J. Alfred Prufrock', 'Portrait of a Lady', 'Rhapsody on a Windy Night' and 'Mr Eliot's Sunday Morning Service').

Biographical Table

In this table are set out the main facts of Eliot's life and the chronology of his writing career.

26 September 1888   Thomas Stearns Eliot born in St. Louis, Missouri; seventh and youngest child of Henry Ware Eliot and Charlotte Chauncey Stearns. The Eliot family is of English origin, the American line descending from Andrew Eliot who came to Massachusetts from East Coker, Somerset in the mid-seventeenth century.

1905   His earliest poetry and prose is published in the *Smith Academy Record*, the school magazine of Smith Academy, St. Louis.

1906   Enters Harvard University, to which he belongs as student, post-graduate and Assistant, studying philosophy, until 1914.

1907–10   Early poetry appears in *The Harvard Advocate*, a student literary magazine of which he was an editor.

1909–11   The period during which were written the earliest pieces in *Selected Poems*: 'Preludes' (1909–11, published July 1915), 'Portrait of a Lady' (1910, published September 1915), 'The Love Song of J. Alfred Prufrock' (1910–11, published June 1915), 'Rhapsody on a Windy Night' (1911, published July 1915).

1910–11	Studies French literature, and philosophy, at the Sorbonne, Paris. So completely does he identify himself with the French that he writes poems in the language and seriously contemplates settling in France. To Munich, August. Returns to Harvard, October.
1914	Arrives in Europe, June; begins study at University of Marburg; threat of war brings him to England in October to Merton College, Oxford, to read Greek philosophy.
1915	Marries Vivienne Haigh-Wood; teaches for one term at a High Wycombe school.
1916	Teaches for four terms at the junior department of Highgate School.
1917	Joins the Foreign Department of Lloyds Bank in the City of London, remaining there for eight years. *Prufrock and Other Observations*, his first volume of poetry, is published in London. Becomes assistant editor of *The Egoist* (a London literary magazine) until 1919.
1919	*Poems*, his second collection published privately. Four of the seven poems in this volume are included in the *Selected Poems* under the head 'Poems 1920'.
1920	*Ara Vos Prec*, his third collection published in London (in New York as *Poems*): contains all the twelve poems included in the *Selected Poems* before *The Waste Land*.
1922	*The Waste Land* published, in London in the October issue of *The Criterion* (the literary magazine Eliot founded, and edited until 1939) and in New York in the November issue of *The Dial*.
1925	Becomes a director of the publishing

	house now known as Faber and Faber. *Poems 1909–1925* published in London and New York.
1927	Joins the Church of England.
1930	*Ash-Wednesday* published in London and New York.
1934	*The Rock* published.
1935	*Murder in the Cathedral* published.
1939	*The Family Reunion* and *Old Possum's Book of Practical Cats* published.
1943	*Four Quartets* published in New York, in 1943, London, 1944. The four poems appeared separately as follows: *Burnt Norton* 1936; *East Coker* 1940; *The Dry Salvages* 1941; *Little Gidding* 1942.
1948	Awarded the Nobel Prize for Literature; received Order of Merit.
1950	*The Cocktail Party* published.
1954	*The Confidential Clerk* published.
1957	Marries Valerie Fletcher.
1959	*The Elder Statesman* published.
4th January 1965	Death in London.

Preface

This Guide must open with a word of explanation. People are rightly suspicious of notes—and this book is made up of little else. Worse still, they are notes that seem to load the reading of poetry with a burden of fact and speculation. But in compiling this Guide my one aim has been to help the reader towards his own understanding of Eliot's poetry in the volume of *Selected Poems*. Basically, this Guide is an aid, to be used like any dictionary or work of reference, to be consulted and then put aside.

It was my original intention to keep the notes quite free of interpretation. But in some cases our recognition of a source, an allusion or some other kind of 'fact' is dependent upon interpretation. So, in the event, it has proved impossible to exclude this speculative element from notes which are primarily factual.

A second intention I have kept to: that is to avoid any direct critical discussion of Eliot's poetic methods. Clearly, this would touch upon questions of organization and unity in poetry which involves a good deal of quotation and external reference. These are questions which arise with every poem. Our view of Eliot's achievement cannot remain unaffected by our knowledge of his areas of reference and allusion, and by our understanding of the uses to which this material is put. These matters are left for the reader to judge for himself.

Note on the 1971 impression: mistakes and misprints have been corrected. I have not altered the references to *The Waste Land* on pages 133–4, although the long-lost manuscript has now come to light. Full details of the poem's revision will be available in the forthcoming text prepared by Mrs. Eliot.

Introduction

'A large part of any poet's "inspiration" must come from his reading and from his knowledge of history.'

T. S. ELIOT, *To-Day*, September 1918

No one, however learned, has ever claimed that Eliot's poetry makes easy reading. This book is designed to elucidate one particular kind of difficulty—the special problems of meaning which face the reader immediately, on the very surface of the poems, in Eliot's use of quotations and allusions, his reference to many languages and literatures, and his implication of a wide range of fact and learning. Sometimes quotation and allusion become the very language of the poetry, as we see at the end of *The Waste Land*, whose closing lines are a mosaic of literary fragments. Sometimes the learning seems to raise a barrier, a literal barrier, as it becomes at the head of 'Burbank', whose epigraph presents us with a maze of scrambled quotations to be penetrated before ever the poem comes into sight.

It is no surprise then that Eliot has been accused of obscurity and pretentiousness. This is the cost of writing difficult poetry, of being judged by readers who have not attempted to test the poet's meaning or analyse his technique. And even some of those who would describe themselves as Eliot admirers are not always prepared to face the demands of sheer knowledge that his poetry makes.

Eliot has himself touched upon the question of difficulty in modern poetry. He said that difficulty is not something peculiar to certain writers, but a condition of writing in the contemporary world. In a context of 'great variety and complexity' the modern poet can only respond with 'various and complex results'. 'The poet must become more and more comprehensive, more allusive, more indirect, in order to force, to dislocate if

INTRODUCTION

necessary, language into his meaning.'[1] Eliot's proposition may sound stern and unsympathetic, likely to produce stern and unsympathetic poetry. But we know that the case is otherwise. Much of his poetry can be read with pleasure at first sight, although not, of course, with immediate and full understanding. Eliot put the matter well. 'I know that some of the poetry to which I am most devoted is poetry which I did not understand at first reading.' He said that he was passionately fond of certain French verse long before he could be confident of translating it. Yet Eliot also insisted that when poetry calls for knowledge, the poetry-lover must be prepared to answer that demand. He found this with Dante's *Divina Commedia* and he advised other readers from his personal experience. 'If you get nothing out of it at first, you probably never will; but if from your first deciphering of it there comes now and then some direct shock of poetic intensity, nothing but laziness can deaden the desire for fuller and fuller knowledge.'

This Guide is to meet precisely this latter instance. It is meant for the reader who has responded to Eliot's poetry and is seeking the means towards fuller knowledge. Essentially, it is designed to serve as a work of reference, to accompany the volume of *Selected Poems* (a selection made by Eliot himself and including the most important poems before the *Four Quartets*). It provides factual information about specific details in the poems—the source of literary quotations, the English meaning of foreign words and phrases, the presence of allusions, the identity of historical figures and events, and definitions for words adapted or invented by Eliot, and for rare or archaic terms usually included only in the largest dictionaries.

Much of this information can be found elsewhere, for many of the critical and interpretative studies of Eliot necessarily

---

[1] This, anyway, was Eliot's theory in 'The Metaphysical Poets' (1921). Other people have argued differently, notably the poet and critic Yvor Winters, who describes Eliot's view as 'the fallacy of expressive, or imitative form'. Winters traces this fallacy back to the theory formulated by Henry Adams, 'that modern art must be chaotic in order to express chaos' (see Winters, *Primitivism and Decadence* (1937), *The Anatomy of Nonsense* (1943)).

INTRODUCTION

deal with matters of fact. However, readers who want to arrive at their own understanding of the poetry may prefer to have the information provided systematically, poem-by-poem, free from critical comment, with no assumptions made about their knowledge of English literature, the Bible, and the other historical and cultural traditions upon which Eliot draws.

The majority of the entries in this Guide cover precise and obvious points. Eliot often signals his use of quotations by italics or quotation marks. Most of the historical and factual references to people and events are equally straightforward and unmistakable. With allusions, however, there cannot be certainty. One reader may see an allusion that another reader denies. So I have tried to exercise restraint and common sense, not searching for allusions, merely identifying those which are obvious and which seem relevant to the poem's meaning.

Sources I have dealt with less exhaustively. By sources I mean the literary or other works by which Eliot's poetry is visibly influenced—in terms, say, of diction, imagery, verse form or subject-matter—to the extent of material obligation. Sometimes the borrowings are obvious and from well-known works; and Eliot would be expecting his reader to recognize these sources and follow his use of them. But sometimes the sources are little-known or obscure. In these cases we can assume that Eliot would not expect or require his reader to identify them; and sometimes, as the poet has admitted, the sources are 'unconscious', inasmuch as the borrowed material came to Eliot's mind without his having any sense of its external origin. To make an exhaustive inquiry into these areas would be an enormous and complex task, and it would take us into literary history and the psychology of creation, well away from points of local and immediate meaning in the poetry.

This question arises, for example, with Eliot's extensive use of the French nineteenth-century symbolist poets, a wide-scale indebtedness which can be seen in much of his poetry up to about 1920. We can detect the influence of Gautier in Eliot's quatrains; of Laforgue (to whom, Eliot said in 1961, he owed 'more than to any one poet in one language'), in the movement and structure of his *vers-libre*; of Rimbaud, Baudelaire, Mallarmé and Corbière. The debt is undeniably extensive—in diction and phrasing, in lines adapted or paraphrased from the French models, in subject-matter and in the attitude of romantic irony which Eliot holds towards the experience of life in cities—'the more sordid aspects of the modern metropolis', whose 'poetical possibilities' he discovered through the poetry of Baudelaire. We have here a remarkable example of the way in which a powerful talent can ingest the materials of others, putting them, directly and indirectly, to an individual use. It is a process that should be studied by anyone who wants to determine the nature of Eliot's originality, to see what contributed to this new voice in English poetry, or who wants to trace the stages in his development. But these insights can be grasped only through an extensive reading of the French poets. An accumulation of source references would merely be cumbersome, and positively obstructive to the reader whose prime use of this book is for the elucidation of specific points in the text.

Another source for one of the earliest poems was Dostoevsky. In the winter of 1910–11, when he was studying in Paris, Eliot read French translations of three of Dostoevsky's novels, *Crime and Punishment*, *The Idiot* and *The Brothers Karamazov*. When an American scholar, John C. Pope, suggested (many years later) that the figure of Prufrock and the poem as a whole bear the impress of Eliot's reading of *Crime and Punishment*, the poet agreed: 'These three novels made a very profound impression on me and I had read them all before *Prufrock* was completed.' About this time Eliot was also reading the works of Charles-Louis Philippe, a novelist particularly concerned with Paris as a city of exhaustion, degradation, poverty and gloom. In 'Preludes' III and IV and in 'Rhapsody on a Windy Night' Eliot draws upon *Bubu-de-Montparnasse* (1898) and *Marie Donadieu* (1904) for certain images and settings. But, as with Eliot's use of Dostoevsky, it would not be enough to refer the reader to specific details; Eliot's response was to the works entire.

I have also omitted any listing of the multitude of possible sources for the passages of pastiche in 'Gerontion' and *The Waste Land*. Eliot's brilliant imitations of Elizabethan and Jacobean dramatic verse evoke for us, in a few lines, the way in which these writers experienced life and the style in which they communicated this experience. Eliot means us to catch this aspect of the past. To investigate the range of sources would distract us from this primary element of meaning.

I have also neglected sources which seem to be trivial or meaningless. For example, in 1919 Eliot reviewed *The Education of Henry Adams* for *The Athenæum*. In the review, he referred to the arrival in England of two Americans, Henry Adams himself in 1858, Henry James in 1870, both of whom, he wrote, 'land at Liverpool and descend at the same hotel'. No one can miss the likeness between these words and the opening lines of 'Burbank':

> Burbank crossed a little bridge
> Descending at a small hotel;
> Princess Volupine arrived,
> They were together, and he fell.

The poem was published (in the summer issue of *Art and Letters*) a month or so after the review; and the phrasing of the review could not have been absent from Eliot's mind. But it would be irresponsible to refer to the review as a significant source. Are we to suppose that Eliot would want us to catch some ironic parallel, or contrast, perhaps, between the arrival at Liverpool of those two highly-civilized and cultivated American writers and the arrival at Venice of the Baedeker-carrying Burbank, a twentieth-century American tourist and the promiscuous Princess with whom he is so unambiguously involved at their same 'small hotel'? The answer may be Yes; that Eliot would expect at least some of the readers of his poem to recall *The Athenæum* for 22nd May 1919, to catch and savour the comic parallel. Perhaps he advised his friends to look out for it. If there is any question of a deliberate reference on Eliot's part, it can only be as a private joke; as may be his use of the adjective 'protrusive' for Bleistein's popping eyes: the word occurs in a passage of Henry Adams quoted in that same review. Such instances tell us about the poet's sense of humour, his associative mind, and his contemporary audience. But they have no relevance to the poem's essential and permanent meaning.

There are other 'Burbank'-*Athenæum* parallels. For example, the issue for 25th April 1919 contains a translation of Cavafy's poem 'The God Abandons Antony'. On 2nd May, there is a reference in a review by Eliot to Shakespeare's 'The Phoenix and the Turtle'. Echoes of the Cavafy title and Shakespeare's poem appear in the second stanza of 'Burbank'. All that we can deduce from this evidence is that traces of Eliot's reading and literary journalism have found their way through to the poem. Similar instances of infiltration are to be found by anyone who searches the files of the periodicals which Eliot contributed to or edited. A comparison between this material and the poetry he was currently writing, might provide an insight upon the process of poetic creation. But it would tell us little or nothing about the public meaning of these poems.

Another instance of what we might term an *irrelevant* source is 'Crapy Cornelia' by Henry James, a short story published in 1909 and probably read then by Eliot, at the time 'Prufrock' was forming in his mind. The story opens to a distinctly Prufrockian note. The forty-eight-year-old bachelor White-Mason is caught in a moment of hesitation, hesitating on a visit he has to make, a question he has to put, a point he has to come to. The 'point', 'the important question', as we are to learn, is a proposal of marriage. The likeness to 'Prufrock' is also in the person of White-Mason as a self-conscious dandy, worried about his age; and the 'etherised' patient image may have been triggered by a reference to ether in the story. Perhaps, as with 'Burbank', Eliot's intimates would have spotted the joke. But 'Prufrock' has a life of its own. Its Jamesian elements—in matters of detail and in a light parody of the novelist's late style—exist only as points of departure, as ingredients, along with Dostoevsky and Charles-Louis Philippe, in a masterpiece which is Eliot's through and through, achieved by a marvellous assumption of the most varied materials. Thus to remark upon

INTRODUCTION

'Crapy Cornelia' as a source is to make a historical and psychological observation rather than a point of meaning.

But the most striking and instructive example of an irrelevant source is found with *The Waste Land*. At some time between 1913 and 1920–21, Eliot must have come across a book now forgotten and at the time little known. This book was *My Past*, the autobiography of the Countess Marie Larisch, published in 1913. It is the reminiscence of an Austrian noblewoman, a niece and favourite of the Austrian Empress Elizabeth, and related to Ludwig II, the 'mad king' of Bavaria. The Countess was not a skilled writer (indeed the memoirs were worked up by that most accomplished of literary ghosts, Maude Ffoulkes); nor a very interesting woman; and the moments of her life were little more than the scandals of the court. Yet there is an undeniable fascination about this briskly-told story of corruption, of sexual intrigue and domestic subterfuge in the royal circles of Europe.

For whatever reason, specific details from *My Past* stuck in Eliot's mind. They came to the surface again in the composition of *The Waste Land*. In the opening verse-paragraph we find unmistakable borrowings and adaptations: Marie's name (line 15) (unusual for central Europe; Maria would be the standard form); the Starnbergersee (line 8), the lake beside which stood one of her childhood homes; an arch-duke cousin (lines 13–14), of whom she had several; wintering in the south (line 18), corresponding to her own moves from Austria to Menton; the feeling of freedom in the mountains (line 17), to which Marie refers several times; an unexpected summer rainstorm (lines 8–9), corresponding to the storm which overtook her and the Empress when they were out riding together. And there are extensive correspondences elsewhere—several passages about death by drowning, many references to Wagner and a striking section on fortune-telling.

The discovery of this source was a matter of pure chance, the observation of an American scholar, Mr. G. K. L. Morris, who happened to come across the book in a French provincial hotel in the early 1950's. But for this fortuitous stroke we might never

INTRODUCTION

have known of this remote source; nor would it have mattered much; for Eliot's use of these details is quite independent of their forgotten origin. Their meaning arises wholly from the context of the poem in which they now stand.

On the other hand, my long note to lines 1 to 18 of *The Waste Land* (see page 72), mentions Rupert Brooke's famous poem 'The Old Vicarage, Grantchester'. This is not, in the strict sense, a source. But it is a work which I am sure Eliot wanted to call to the reader's mind. He evokes it through verbal, structural and thematic echoes. Eliot asserts the large and essential difference between the experience of life in *The Waste Land*, a subtle and complex experience, and Rupert Brooke's relatively simple, single view. To put the issue briefly: *My Past* is irrelevant to the meaning of *The Waste Land* for all that it supplies considerable detail; it is an *accidental* source. Whereas 'The Old Vicarage, Grantchester' is a parallel we are required to keep in sight, not as a source, but as a term of reference, one aspect of Eliot's meaning.

As a general rule interpretation is left to the reader. Most of the notes simply carry the information relevant to single points in the text. The two occasions where it has seemed necessary and helpful to break this rule are in the prefatory sections to *The Waste Land* and 'The Hollow Men'. In the latter, there is a brief note on Dante's *Divina Commedia*, possibly the most important single note in the entire Guide.

To read Eliot in ignorance of Dante is to neglect a dimension of meaning that the poet exploits throughout his major works. The opening words of 'Prufrock' take their point from the Dante epigraph. Prufrock is conducting us through the realm of a twentieth-century Inferno and Purgatory; and in this and other poems, including the *Four Quartets*, Eliot relates the experience of modern man to the experience of mankind given to us in Dante's prodigious statement. In calling his third collection of poems *Ara Vos Prec*, Eliot was trying to compel an informed response from his contemporary readers. How many of them could recognize the language as Provençal? the source as the *Purgatorio* xxvi? If they were unable to catch the allusion,

Eliot was forcing them (at least, those with inquiring minds) to familiarize themselves with the *Divina Commedia*.

In providing notes to *The Waste Land* he was more positively helpful. Eliot brings the allusions to our notice. They cannot be ignored. The poet explained this quite clearly in a talk, 'What Dante means to Me', given in 1950. 'Readers of my *Waste Land* will perhaps remember that the vision of my city clerks trooping over London Bridge from the railway station to their offices evoked the reflection "I had not thought death had undone so many" [line 63]; and that in another place I deliberately modified a line of Dante by altering it—"Sighs, short and infrequent, were exhaled" [line 64]. And I gave the references in my notes, in order to make the reader who recognized the allusion, know that I meant him to recognize it, and to know that he would have missed the point if he did not recognize it.'

In the same talk Eliot paid his tribute to Dante as 'the most persistent and deepest influence' on his poetry. He has described his method: 'I have borrowed lines from him, in the attempt to reproduce, or rather to arouse in the reader's mind the memory, of some Dantesque scene, and thus establish a relationship between the medieval inferno and modern life.' It is an influence whose effect cannot be assessed by cataloguing references and allusions. Dante's thought, the simplicity and beauty of his language, the clarity and force of his images, the shape of his verse, all of these are felt anew in Eliot, and anyone coming fresh to the Italian poet can make no better start than by reading Eliot's 'Dante' essay of 1929, which tells us so warmly and lucidly of his response to Dante's art.

A second work to which I would draw the reader's attention is the story 'Heart of Darkness' by Joseph Conrad, also referred to in the prefatory section to 'The Hollow Men'. Conrad's nightmare vision would have made sense to Dante; and one would judge that these two writers were felt by Eliot to exert a single force flowing into and empowering his imagination.

A full understanding of Eliot's poetry involves us in wide and serious reading. But seriousness should not lead us into solemnity. The author of *The Waste Land* was the same man who wrote that hilariously grotesque satire 'The Hippopotamus' and the charming fantasies in *Old Possum's Book of Practical Cats* (1939). Another expression of wit is seen in the thicket of quotations at the head of 'Burbank', a kind of intellectual puzzle, challenging the reader to identify its parts and to relate them to the poem they head. Or 'Mr. Eliot's Sunday Morning Service', a satire on pedantry, defiantly pedantic in its glancing references to the disputes of the early Christian church and in its comically obscure diction, a parody of the language of scholasticism. Eliot means us to admire and smile, to enjoy the lightness and skill with which he can turn his learning to a joke, to glimpse a poet-dandy, the virtuoso delighting with us in the flourish of his own performance.

Eliot's most elaborate joke concerns us directly in the use of this Guide, for it involves the notes he provided to *The Waste Land*. At a public lecture given at the University of Minnesota in 1956, Eliot explained that the notes he had originally set down on the manuscript were only source references, intended as a safeguard against the accusation of plagiarism, a charge that had been made against his earlier poetry. But when *The Waste Land* was first printed in 1922 it was without notes of any kind (it came out in two periodicals, in London and New York). The notes were added to the first book edition, published in the same year, to oblige the publisher Liveright (of the New York firm of Boni and Liveright) who 'wanted a larger volume and the notes were the only available matter' (as Eliot explained elsewhere).

Recounting this, Eliot remarked that over the years the notes 'have had almost greater popularity than the poem itself', a nice enough joke. But perhaps some members of that university audience, and scholars elsewhere, when they later read the printed version of the lecture in 1957, may have been rather less amused by his discomforting account of the notes as a 're-markable exposition of bogus scholarship' which he had often thought of omitting. Of course, the joke works both ways. Some of the notes are very far from being 'bogus scholarship', or at

INTRODUCTION

least they are good explication. The note to line 218 is our most important guide to the reading of the poem, to its fluid categories; the first part of the note to line 279 is extremely helpful; and without the note to line 433 Eliot's use of the word 'Shantih' would be incomprehensible.

None the less, many of the notes are bait for the unwary. In presenting them, Eliot shows little regard for accuracy or relevance, as if he is really indifferent to whether or not the reader uses them. The compiler of this Guide took the trouble to track down the work referred to so summarily in Eliot's note to line 264. P. S. King and Son Ltd. turn out not to be the publishers, trade sponsors or authors but the agents of sale for a London County Council official report by the Council's Clerk and Architect. Some of the notes are personal asides, endearing, yet unhelpful, as to line 360, where Eliot confides to us that he has forgotten the precise account of the Antarctic expedition, 'but I think one of Shackleton's'. Or the amusing mock-pedantry of line 357, quoting from Chapman's *Handbook of Birds of Eastern North America* for the habitat of the hermit-thrush, the *Turdus aonalaschkae pallasii.*

If nothing else, these mock-notes are a useful reminder to us of the poet's presence, of a personality with individual quirks and a distinctive point of view. They remind us too that the author can properly regard his sources as playthings, to be followed verbatim, or imitated, or changed at will. Mario Praz has suggested that this is the case in Eliot's use of certain images in Dante: 'It is as if Eliot had been reading Dante without giving much heed to the meaning, but letting himself be impressed by a few clear visual images: these he rearranges in his own mind just as in a kaleidoscope the same coloured glasses can give a no less harmonious (though different) design than the previous one.' Eliot himself raises this question in *The Use of Poetry and the Use of Criticism*, discussing an astrological image in 'Gerontion' which he originally found in a play by the Elizabethan dramatist George Chapman (see pages 46–7, note to lines 67–9), who in turn probably took it from the Roman playwright Seneca. Eliot speculated, from his own experience, that 'this imagery had some personal saturation value, so to speak, for Seneca; another for Chapman, and another for myself. . . .' He stressed that the feelings awakened by the imagery were possibly 'too obscure for the authors to know quite what they were'.

In discussing the astrological image in 'Gerontion', Eliot went on to point to another unfathomable mystery surrounding the source of imagery:

> Only a part of an author's imagery comes from his reading. It comes from the whole of his sensitive life since early childhood. Why, for all of us, out of all that we have heard, seen, felt, in a lifetime, do certain images recur, charged with emotion, rather than others? . . . six ruffians seen through an open window playing cards at night at a small French railway junction where there was a water-mill: such memories may have a symbolic value, but of what we cannot tell, for they come to represent the depths of feeling into which we cannot peer.

In the 'Journey of the Magi' we encounter these images again, now set in a time and place remote from twentieth-century France. I have quoted these examples in order to emphasize the areas of knowledge which are beyond the scope of any handbook, and to underline the fact that our surest guide in interpreting the use to which Eliot puts his sources is our own sense of his habits of mind, a context of meaning to be discovered in the poems themselves, not through notes.

In the passage I have just quoted, Eliot draws our attention to images, deriving from experiences in his own life, which carry a density of meaning that he is unable to explain. This accords with a central tenet in his theory of poetic creation: 'the more perfect the artist, the more completely separate in him will be the man who suffers and the mind which creates. . . . It is not in his personal emotions, the emotions provoked by particular events in his life, that the poet is in any way remarkable or interesting . . . *significant* emotion, emotion which has its life in the poem and not in the history of the poet. The emotion of art is impersonal' ('Tradition and the Individual

INTRODUCTION

Talent', 1919). The force of these remarks should restrain us from interpreting Eliot's poetry through the details of his life; and, in practice, these details are not needed for the understanding of his work. Nevertheless, there is some point in knowing that correspondences do exist, that places and people in real life were carried through, sometimes much modified or fragmented, to the poetry; that, for example, Eliot probably saw the name Prufrock-Littau, furniture-wholesalers, on advertisements in his hometown of St. Louis, Missouri; that Sweeney was a figure probably derived from Eliot's recollection of the Irish ex-pugilist with whom he took boxing lessons at Boston during his student days at Harvard; that the lines

> On Margate Sands.
> I can connect
> Nothing with nothing.

in *The Waste Land* were written when Eliot was actually at Margate, convalescing from a breakdown and finding it difficult to write, for three weeks in October and November 1921.

I have allowed myself some freedom in including occasional historical or biographical notes which may seem remote from questions of meaning in the text. These touch on issues which I believe to be generally helpful in our understanding of the inspiration and nature of Eliot's poetry. Such, for example, is the very first note in the book, treating the dedication to *Prufrock and Other Observations* and in particular the identity of the dedicatee, Jean Verdenal. Although we know virtually nothing about him, the dedication establishes clearly enough his importance to the poet, both as a friend and as one killed in the war, one of Eliot's own generation. There remained for Eliot, as he recalled in 1934, a precious memory of Verdenal 'coming across the Luxembourg Gardens in the late afternoon, waving a branch of lilac', a scene which belongs to when he knew him in Paris before the war. Can this image have been far from Eliot's mind when he wrote the opening lines of *The Waste Land*, and placed them beneath the title 'The Burial of the

Dead'? This, of course, is pure speculation. But *The Waste Land*, for all its constructedness and intellectual design, reads as the creation of a poet who has suffered his own 'waste land'. It is a poem 'reticent, yet confessional' (Harriet Monroe's phrase for Eliot's poetry in general); and before its publication he wrote to his mother that the poem contained much of his life. This should not set us off on a futile and destructive search for personal clues. Nevertheless, its attachment to Eliot's life is a dimension of its meaning, and this we should attend to, however lightly and tactfully; and if I seem to take up the question rather heavy-handedly it is perhaps in response to Eliot's own insistence upon the impersonality of art and the semblance of impersonality that so much of his poetry successfully conveys.

And, in more general terms, we should not forget the importance to Eliot of his American origins. A man of European culture, he was still able to say of his poetry—'in its sources, in its emotional springs, it comes from America'.

The truth which Eliot could never escape from, whether by poetic artifice or prose argument, is neatly put by Thoreau: 'Poetry is a piece of very private history, which unostentatiously lets us into the secret of a man's life.' With this in mind, I have not altogether excluded biographical references from the notes, although they are not essential to the public meaning of the poetry. In Eliot's choice of the name Prufrock, the origin is a purely accidental factor. What is significant is the range of verbal associations which the name awakens —prudence, primness, prissiness (and so on)—associations which seem to be answered by the character of the man who reveals himself in the poem. Eliot is playing off the slightly absurd ring of J. Alfred Prufrock against the romantic expectations aroused by the words *The Love Song of*; it is a joke against the convention that Love Songs are not the preserve of people with such laughably unromantic names. To catch this significance in the name and in the poem's title, the reader has to do his own thinking. It is not an instance where factual or historical notes will help. Another case is Pipit, the mysterious someone in 'A Cooking Egg'. Who is she? Our sense of her identity will affect our understanding of the poem. But one's own guess is as good as anyone else's. The critics cannot agree. An old aunt? a former nurse or governess? a childhood playmate, now visited many years later? a mistress? These are the suggestions.

In this trivial instance the reader must judge the evidence and come to his own conclusions, exactly as he must throughout his reading of Eliot. Freedom is our prerogative. Eliot pointed this out in commenting on a collection of essays entitled *Interpretations* (one of which provided an analysis of 'Prufrock'). He drew attention to the fallacy—

> of assuming that there must be just one interpretation of the poem as a whole, that must be right . . . as for the meaning of the poem as a whole, it is not exhausted by any explanation, for the meaning is what the poem means to different sensitive readers.

Or we can remember his response to an inquiry about the meaning of a much debated line in *Ash-Wednesday*, 'Lady, three white leopards sat under a juniper-tree.' Eliot answered, 'I mean . . .' and simply read back the line to his questioner without any comment whatsoever. The implication for this Guide is clear. Beyond the level of mere information, no external aid is of final use to us in our reading of T. S. Eliot or any other poet; and the sooner we are able to dispense with the aid that this book represents, the sooner we are able to read the poetry directly and fully, by way of a personal encounter. Our real understanding of the poetry, and of the poet, begins where these notes end.

B.C.S.

Note on Dating

For readers interested in tracing the course of Eliot's development in these poems, I have added the dates and places of composition, where these are known. I have also given details of their first publication. These indicate the circulation the poems enjoyed.

The details of composition I have checked with two works whose authors consulted Eliot: E. J. H. Greene, *T. S. Eliot et la France* (Paris, 1951) and W. J. Pope, 'The Early Works of T. S. Eliot' (unpublished M.A. thesis, University of London, 1950). I also referred to a French edition, *Poèmes 1910–1930* (Paris, 1947), whose editor, Pierre Leyris, was advised by John Hayward, an intimate friend of the poet and knowledgeable on such matters. The full bibliographical details are to be found in Donald Gallup, *T. S. Eliot, A Bibliography* (1952, rev. ed. 1969).

PRUFROCK AND OTHER OBSERVATIONS

Dedication: Jean Verdenal was a friend whom Eliot knew in Paris in 1910–11. He was killed on the Anglo-French expedition to the Dardanelles early in 1915.

The lines, from Dante (*Purgatorio*, xxi, 133–6), are a testimony to the strength of their friendship; they are taken from what Eliot described as one of the most 'affecting' meetings in the poem. Dante is being conducted through the underworld by the spirit of the Roman poet Virgil, who is recognized by the spirit of another Roman poet, Statius, one of his followers. Statius stoops and tries to grasp Virgil's feet in homage. But Virgil stops him with the reminder that they are both insubstantial shadows. Eliot quotes Statius's answer: 'Now can you understand the quantity of love that warms me towards you, so that I forget our vanity, and treat the shadows like the solid thing.' (The translation of these lines, as in many of these Dante quotations in this Guide, is that used by Eliot in his 'Dante' essay (1929).)

Eliot referred again to his friendship with Verdenal, many years later, in *The Criterion* for April 1934, comparing the richness of Paris as against the cultural 'deserts' of England and America: 'I am willing to admit that my own retrospect is touched by a sentimental sunset, the memory of a friend coming across the Luxembourg Gardens in the late afternoon, waving a branch of lilac, a friend who was later (so far as I could find out) to be mixed with the mud of Gallipoli.'

THE LOVE SONG OF
J. ALFRED PRUFROCK

Written Paris, Munich 1910–11; Poetry *(Chicago) June 1915*

Epigraph: 'If I thought that my reply would be to someone who would ever return to earth, this flame would remain without further movement; but as no one has ever returned alive from this gulf, if what I hear is true, I can answer you with no fear of infamy.' These words are spoken by Count Guido de Montefeltrano (1223–98) in Dante's *Inferno* xxvii, 61–6. Dante recounts his visit to the underworld. In the Eighth Chasm of Hell he meets Guido, punished here, with other false and deceitful counsellors, in a single prison of flame for his treacherous advice on earth to Pope Boniface. When the damned speak from this flame, the voice sounds from the tip, which trembles. Guido refers to this, and goes on to explain that he speaks freely only because he believes that Dante is like himself, one of the dead, who will never return to earth to report what he says.

l. 14 Michelangelo: (1475–1564), great Italian sculptor, painter and poet.

ll. 23–48: In this section Eliot places considerable emphasis on the phrase 'there will be time' and variants upon it, echoing the words of the preacher in Ecclesiastes iii, 1–8: 'To every thing there is a season, and a time to every purpose under the heaven: A time to be born, and a time to die; a time to plant, and a time to pluck up that which is planted; A time to kill, and a time to heal; a time to break down and a time to build up; A time to weep, and a time to laugh; a time to mourn, and a time to dance . . . a time to keep silence, and a time to speak.'

l. 23: cf. 'Had we but world enough and time', from the poem 'To His Coy Mistress' by Andrew Marvell (1621–78). The poet argues to his 'coy mistress' there would be time for delay only if their opportunities for love-making were endless.

l. 29 works and days: echoes the title 'Works and Days', a poem by the Greek writer Hesiod (8th century B.C.). It contains an account of primitive conditions in the country, together with maxims and practical instructions adapted to the peasant's life.

l. 52 a dying fall: cf. 'That strain again! It had a dying fall.' These are the words of Duke Orsino in Shakespeare's *Twelfth Night* I, i. He is love-sick; the music suits his mood and he orders an encore.

l. 60 butt-ends: an image based on the butts or ends of smoked cigarettes.

ll. 63–4: cf. 'A bracelet of bright hair about the bone' in 'The Relique' by John Donne (1572–1631), a line whose 'powerful effect' Eliot remarks upon in 'The Metaphysical Poets' (1921).

ll. 73–4: cf. 'for you yourself, sir, should be old as I am, if like a crab you could go backwards'. The words of Hamlet in Shakespeare's *Hamlet* II, ii. He is simulating madness and addresses the old courtier Polonius. There are further references to *Hamlet* in lines 111, 117–18, 119.

l. 81: This line has a Biblical ring (cf. 'they mourned, and wept and fasted,' 2 Samuel i, 12; and 'I fasted and wept,' xii, 21), perhaps in anticipation of the Biblical allusion of the following line.

ll. 82–3: John the Baptist was decapitated and his head brought into Herod's court by Salome. Herod presented it to her as a reward for her dancing before him. The story is told in Mark vi, 17–29; Matthew xiv, 3–11.

l. 92: cf. 'Let us roll all our strength, and all/Our sweetness, up into one ball.' At the close of 'To His Coy Mistress' (see note to line 23) the poet urges his beloved to enjoy love with him urgently and intensely.

ll. 94–5: Two Lazaruses are mentioned in the Bible. One was the brother of Mary and Martha, the dead man whom Christ brought back to life, whose story is told in John xi, 1–44. This Lazarus said nothing of his experience. The other Lazarus is the beggar associated with the rich man Dives, in the parable told in Luke xvi, 19–31. When they died, the poor man went to heaven, the rich man to hell. Dives wanted to warn his five brothers what hell was like, so he asked God if Lazarus could be sent back to tell them. But God refused: 'if they hear not Moses and the prophets, neither will they be persuaded, though one rose from the dead.'

l. 95: 'to tell all' will be to do as Christ promised of the Holy Ghost: 'he shall teach you all things, and bring all things to your remembrance' (John xiv, 26).

l. 111 Prince Hamlet: the hero of *Hamlet*, the opening of whose best-known soliloquy, 'To be or not to be' III, i), is echoed at the end of this line. Hamlet was given to self-scrutiny and tormented by indecisiveness. Thus Prufrock's sudden exclamation is to cut short the Hamlet-like soliloquy he has just indulged in and to assert his own subordinate, unheroic role in life.

l. 117 Full of high sentence: cf. 'ful of hy sentence', meaning full of lofty sentiments and learned talk, a description of the conversation of the scholarly Clerk of Oxford in the General Prologue (l. 306) of *The Canterbury Tales* by Geoffrey Chaucer (1343?–1400).

ll. 117–19: a description that calls to mind the long-winded and moralizing Polonius (see note to ll. 73–4).

l. 119 Fool: The Fool was a stock character in Elizabethan drama. He was often a court entertainer whose patter, seeming nonsense, contained a paradoxical wisdom. The court jester in *Hamlet* was Yorick; Hamlet remembers him (now dead twenty-three years) from his boyhood with affection and pity (see v, i).

l. 120: see note to lines 73–4.

l. 121: these would be trousers with turn-ups, then just coming into fashion.

l. 122 Shall I part my hair behind?: In his autobiographical essay *Ushant* (1952), Eliot's Harvard contemporary Conrad Aiken tells us what a sensation was caused when one of their fellow-students returned from Paris 'in exotic Left Bank clothing, and with his hair parted behind'. Clearly, at the time, such a hair-style was regarded as daringly bohemian.

l. 124: cf. 'Teach me to heare Mermaides singing', from 'Song' by John Donne. This is one of a series of challenges, richly poetic, yet unattainable.

PORTRAIT OF A LADY

Written 1910–11; Others *(New York) September 1915*

The American poet and novelist Conrad Aiken, a close friend of Eliot at Harvard, identifies the Lady of this poem as a Harvard hostess, 'our dear deplorable friend, Miss X, the *précieuse ridicule* to end all preciosity, serving tea so exquisitely among her bric-a-brac'. In his autobiographical essay, *Ushant* (1952), Aiken indicates that there are aspects of the poet himself in the poem: 'the oh so precious, the oh so exquisite, Madelaine, the Jamesian lady of ladies, the enchantress of the Beacon Hill drawing-room . . . was afterwards to be essentialized and ridiculed (and his own pose with it) in the Tsetse's *Portrait d'une Femme*.'

Title: Echoes that of the novel *The Portrait of a Lady* (1881) by Henry James, and the poem itself is remarkably Jamesian in its tones and ironies, the subtlety of its observation and in the style of the dialogue.

Epigraph: a snatch of dialogue from *The Jew of Malta* (IV, i) by Christopher Marlowe (1564–93). The first line is spoken by a Friar. He is beginning to accuse Barabas (the villainous Jew of the title), who interrupts him and finishes off the sentence with his own words. It is a scene of double deception. The Friar is trying to blackmail Barabas, not simply charging him with sin. In turn, Barabas's self-accusation is callous and comically prompt. He wants to lead on the Friar by advertising himself as a sinner. In fact, his sins go far deeper. He comes fresh from a grotesque crime—the poisoning of a convent of nuns.

36

PORTRAIT OF A LADY

l. 6 Juliet's tomb: in Shakespeare's *Romeo and Juliet* the tomb is the vault in which Juliet's body is placed, her family supposing her to be dead. Actually, she is only in a coma, drugged, in an attempt to escape an arranged marriage and save herself for Romeo. But the plan goes tragically wrong. Romeo is killed and Juliet commits suicide over his body.

l. 9 Preludes: a group of piano pieces by the Polish composer Frederic Chopin (1810–49).

l. 15 velleities: light inclinations.

l. 28 cauchemar: French for nightmare.

l. 53 buried life: 'The Buried Life' by Matthew Arnold (1822–88) seems to be the source of this phrase. In Arnold, the 'buried life' is 'the mystery of this heart which beats so wild, so deep in us'—the impulsive, passionate side of human nature that we so often try to ignore or suppress. Throughout the 'Portrait' Eliot seems to suppose the reader's acquaintance with 'The Buried Life', on which he provides a kind of modern commentary, a re-writing of Arnold's serious dramatic monologue as a *conversation galante*, a complex statement, with shifting tones of irony, quite different from the relative simplicity of Arnold's singleness of tone and feeling.

l. 122 'dying fall': see page 34, note to 'Prufrock' line 52.

PRELUDES

Written: I, II Harvard 1910; III Paris July 1911; IV Paris 1911

For Eliot's use in these poems of the novels of Charles-Louis Philippe, see the Introduction, page 18; more detailed references are to be found in Grover Smith, *T. S. Eliot's Poetry and Plays*.

RHAPSODY ON A WINDY NIGHT

Written Paris 1911; Blast *(London) July 1915*

Details in this poem—including the sight of the street-lamps, the woman in the doorway, the smells, the memories—are derived from the novel *Bubu-de-Montparnasse* (1898) by Charles-Louis Philippe (see Introduction, p. 18).

ll. 35–40: These lines seem to be based upon a prose-poem by Baudelaire, 'Le Joujou du Pauvre' ('The Urchin's Plaything'). *l. 51:* 'The moon harbours no ill-feelings.' Eliot's line is a version of two lines from 'Complainte de cette bonne lune' ('The Lament of that beautiful Moon') by Jules Laforgue (1860–87): 'Là, voyons mam'zell' la Lune,/Ne gardons pas ainsi rancune' ('Look, there we can see that fine young lady the moon, let's not harbour any ill-feelings').

POEMS 1920

GERONTION

Written London 1919; London 1920

Early in 1922 Eliot was undecided whether or not to print this poem as a prelude to *The Waste Land*. Ezra Pound advised against it and the two poems were kept apart.

Title: a transliteration of the Greek word for little old man.

Epigraph: from Shakespeare's *Measure for Measure* III, i. The Duke is addressing Claudio, a young man sentenced to death, telling him to value life lightly.

ll. 1–2: Eliot wrote in 1938 that 'the line in *Gerontion* was lifted bodily from a Life of Edward Fitzgerald'. In point of fact, these two lines derive from the biography *Edward FitzGerald* (1905), by A. C. Benson, where the poet is described, in Benson's summary of a letter from FitzGerald, as sitting 'in a dry month, old and blind, being read to by a country boy, longing for rain' (p. 142).

l. 3 hot gates: a literal translation of the Greek place-name Thermopylae, a strategically important pass between Northern and Central Greece, the scene of several battles, notably that between the Greeks and Persians in 480 B.C.

l. 9 estaminet: a French word for café, brought into English by soldiers returning from France and Belgium during the First World War.

ll. 9–10 Antwerp, Brussels: these towns, in Belgium, may be connected with London as trading and financial centres.

l. 12 stonecrop: a moss-like plant.　　*merds:* excreta.

l. 14 gutter: a spluttering fire.

GERONTION

l. 17 'We ... sign!': the cry of the unbelieving Pharisees, calling upon Christ to prove his divinity by performing a miracle: 'Master, we would see a sign from thee' (Matthew xii, 38). Christ answered that 'an evil and adulterous generation seeketh after a sign' (39).

ll. 18–19: Eliot's source for this metaphor is a Nativity Sermon preached before James I by Bishop Lancelot Andrewes (1555–1626) on Christmas Day 1618; his text for the sermon was the cry of the Pharisees quoted in line 16. 'Verbum infans, the Word without a word; the eternal Word not able to speak a word: a wonder sure and . . . swaddled; and that a wonder too. He that takes the sea "and rolls it about the swaddling bands of darkness", to come thus into clouts, Himself!' ('clouts' the baby's swaddling clothes).

Andrewes and Eliot both use 'word' in its original Greek sense of *Logos,* as in John i, 1: 'In the beginning was the Word, and the word was with God, and the Word was God.'

l. 19 juvescence: Eliot's version of juvenescence, here meaning the Spring.

l. 20 Christ the tiger: In the poem 'The Tiger' by William Blake (1757–1827) God's aspect of power and wrath, and of mercy and gentleness are manifested in his creation of the tiger and the lamb.

l. 21: this line is a concentrated allusion to a passage in *The Education of Henry Adams* (1918) where Adams describes the strange, pagan richness (as it seemed to him, brought up in bleaker New England) of the Maryland spring: 'The Potomac and its tributaries squandered beauty. . . . Here and there a Negro log cabin alone disturbed the dogwood and the judas-tree. . . . The brooding heat of the profligate vegetation; the cool charm of the running water; the terrific splendour of the June thundergust in the deep and solitary woods, were all sensual, animal, elemental. No European spring had shown him the same intermixture of delicate grace and passionate depravity that marked the Maryland May. He loved it too much as if it were Greek and half human' (p. 268).

44

GERONTION

Eliot himself expressed amazement when years later the scholar F. O. Mathiessen drew his attention to this echo.

l. 22: refers to the presence of Christ in the sacrament of communion, the bread his body, the wine his blood, to be consumed in the mass by the priest and congregation.

l. 24 Limoges: a French town famed for its china.

l. 26 Titians: the paintings of the Venetian artist Titian (d. 1576).

ll. 29–30: an allusion to the lamentation of Job, whose days were passed in suffering and for whom life had lost its meaning: 'My days are swifter than a weaver's shuttle, and are spent without hope. O remember that my life is wind: mine eye shall no more see good' (vii,6–7).

ll. 33–69: in this section Eliot is exploiting a wide range of Elizabethan and Jacobean dramatic verse. For reasons set out in the Introduction (see pages 18–19), the full extent of possible sources or models is not listed here, but Eliot's adaptive process can be illustrated through a single example, lines 55–8. The original Eliot seems to have had in mind is eight lines from *The Changeling* by Thomas Middleton (1580–1627):

> I that am of your blood was taken from you
> For your better health; look no more upon 't,
> But cast it to the ground regardlessly,
> Let the common sewer take it from distinction.
> Beneath the stars, upon yon meteor
> Ever hung my fate, 'mongst things corruptible;
> I ne'er could ·pluck it from him; my loathing
> Was prophet to the rest, but ne'er believed.

> (v, iii.)

Eliot quoted these lines in his essay 'Thomas Middleton' (1927), prefacing them with this comment: 'He has no message; he is merely a great recorder. Incidentally, in flashes and when the dramatic need comes, he is a great poet, a great master of versification.'

l. 34 contrived corridors: Eliot may have had a specific contemporary 'contrived corridor' in mind—the so-called Polish Corridor. This was a strip of land taken from Germany under the terms of the Treaty of Versailles (signed June 1919) and awarded to Poland. It was the most resented of the Treaty settlements.

ll. 34–47: This view of history owes much to Eliot's reading of *The Education of Henry Adams*, particularly the sections where Adams discusses the increasing complexity of human knowledge, as in the area of evolution: at the beginning of the twentieth century the historian 'entered a far vaster universe, where all the old roads ran about in every direction, overrunning, dividing, subdividing, stopping abruptly, vanishing slowly, with side-paths that led nowhere, and sequences that could not be proved' (p. 400).

l. 47 the wrath-bearing tree: probably an allusion to 'the tree of knowledge of good and evil' in Genesis; 'wrath-bearing' in that Eve's disobedience in taking from it the forbidden fruit was one reason for the descent of God's wrath upon mankind.

l. 52 concitation: Eliot derives this from the Latin *concitatio*, meaning moving, exciting.

ll. 64–5: an arrangement of mirrors to enable a voluptuary to see himself enacting his pleasures from a variety of angles. Eliot probably had in mind the words of Sir Epicure Mammon in Ben Jonson's play *The Alchemist* (1612):

> my glasses
> Cut in more subtle angles, to disperse
> And multiply the figures, as I walk
> Naked between my succubae.   (ii, i.)

Eliot quoted a passage containing three of these four lines in his essay 'Ben Jonson', published in 1919.

ll. 67–9: In *The Use of Poetry and the Use of Criticism* (1933), pages 146–7, Eliot explained that the imagery in these lines derives from a passage in the play *Bussy D'Ambois* by George Chapman (1559–1634). It is the dying speech of Bussy. He commands his 'fame' to warn the heavens of his coming:

GERONTION

Fly where the evening from the Iberian vales
Takes on her swarthy shoulders Hecate
Crowned with a grove of oaks; fly where men feel
The burning axletree, and those that suffer
Beneath the chariot of the snowy Bear . . .   (v, iv.)

Chapman is drawing upon the classical tradition that sinners
were punished by being sent into an eccentric, outward orbit
which would carry them away into space. The bear (usually
known as the Great Bear) is a constellation in the Northern
hemisphere. For Eliot's remarks on the personal value to him
of this image, see the Introduction, pages 25–6.

l. 70 Belle Isle: an island in the North Atlantic.

   Horn: Cape Horn, the southern extremity of South America.

l. 71 Gulf: the Gulf Stream is a system of currents in the North
Atlantic.

l. 72 Trades: the Trade winds.

BURBANK WITH A BAEDEKER:
BLEISTEIN WITH A CIGAR

Written 1919; Art and Letters *(London) Summer 1919*

Title: Baedeker: Baedeker's guide-books are famed and joked about for their potted entries which enable the tourist to inform himself in the space of a few lines on matters cultural, historical, geographical etc.

Bleistein: German-Jewish name, literally Leadstone. Eliot could have seen the name over a furrier's shop (see line 24) in Upper Thames Street in the City of London.

Epigraph: Tra . . . laire: this is a version of 'Tra la, tra la, la, la la laire', the opening line of the poem 'Sur les Lagunes' ('On the Lagoons') from a group of poems entitled *Variations sur le Carneval de Venise (Variations on the Carnival of Venice)* by Théophile Gautier (1811–72). 'The Carnival of Venice' is a popular traditional tune; it reminds Gautier, at the close of his poem, of

> The city joyous, free and light
> Of Canaletto's day

a detail to which Eliot may be alluding in line 19.

nil . . . fumus: 'only the divine endures; the rest is smoke'. This inscription (the first word is actually 'nihil') is in a painting of the martyrdom of St. Sebastian by Mantegna (1431–1506) in the Ca d'oro, Venice. The words (source unknown) are on a scroll round a guttering candle, a detail to which Eliot may be alluding in line 20. Mantegna was Eliot's favourite artist and he knew this painting when it hung in the house of the Franchetti family on the Grand Canal in Venice.

the gondola . . . pink: the words come from chapter one of *The Aspern Papers* (1888) by Henry James. The reference to the

palace becomes clear in the original version; this is nar-
rated by an American visitor to Venice, whose companion is
an American woman resident in the city: 'The gondola
stopped, the old palace was there; it was a house of the class
which in Venice carries even in extreme dilapidation the digni-
fied name. "How charming! It's grey and pink!" my companion exclaimed.'

Eliot's telescoped version of this passage is not taken directly
from James but from a pastiche quotation put together by
Ford Madox Ford in *Henry James, A Critical Study* (1913), p.
141. *The Aspern Papers* is also related, more generally, to the
Venetian aspect of 'Burbank'. Eliot said that James's method
in the story—'to make a place real not descriptively but by
something happening there'—was the example which led him
to compress so many moments of Venice's past into his own
poem.

goats and monkeys: an explosive outburst by Othello in Shakespeare's *Othello* IV, i, a play largely set in Venice. Othello has
been goaded by Iago into a jealous fury against his Venetian
wife Desdemona and her supposed lover. The animals he
swears by are those traditionally associated with rankness and
lust. In *Henry James* (pp. 140, 143), Ford twice quotes the final
words of James's story 'The Madonna of the Future': 'Cats and
monkeys, monkeys and cats—all human life is there!' Thus
Eliot may be wishing to evoke James as well as *Othello*.

with such hair too!: a phrase from the final stanza of 'A Toccata
of Galuppi's' by Robert Browning (1812–89). The poem is
about the vitality and wonder of life and its destruction in age
and decay. Browning invokes the memory of the Venetian
composer Galuppi (1706–85), associating him with Venice as a
city of youth and love, of great traditions and prosperity. Yet
(says the speaker of this dramatic narrative) the toccata itself is
'cold', the composer a mathematical, scientific man. This train
of association leads him on to thoughts of the decay and death
of those who once enjoyed beauty and riches—'Dear dead
women, with such hair, too.'

so . . . departed: these words are the stage directions which close

49

the *Entertainement of Alice, Dowager Countess of Derby* by John Marston (1575?–1634). The masque is Marston's graceful and flattering tribute to the Countess, his patron. In classical myth, Niobe was the mother who boasted that her children were better than the offspring of Zeus, king of the gods; in the masque, she withdraws in favour of the Countess.

l. 4: cf. 'They were together, and she fell', a line from 'The Sisters', a poem by Alfred Tennyson (1809–93). Eliot's 'he' is an ironic variant; in 'The Sisters', the 'she' is a beautiful girl seduced by an Earl.

l. 5 Defunctive music: funeral music. Shakespeare uses this phrase in 'The Phoenix and the Turtle', a memorial poem for the passing of love and constancy symbolized by the death in a 'mutual flame' of the mythical phoenix and the turtle-dove.

ll. 5–8: a reference to Shakespeare's *Antony and Cleopatra* iv, iii. It is just before the battle of Actium, where Caesar routs the Egyptian forces. A group of Cleopatra's soldiers hears mysterious music. ' 'Tis the god Hercules, whom Antony lov'd Now leaves him,' says one, interpreting the sound as an omen of the defeat to come. Antony, once the man of action, justly loses the patronage of the god of strength, for he has abandoned war for the sake of life with Cleopatra.

ll. 9–11: these lines refer to the rising of the sun. From Venice, it would be seen to rise over the peninsula of Istria, eastwards, across the Adriatic Sea. In classical myth, the sun was figured as a chariot drawn across the sky by a team of horses. Eliot's phrasing, 'Beat . . . with even feet' echoes the words of Horace 'aequo pulsat pede' (*Odes* I, iv, 13) describing the movement of death among all mankind, kings and paupers alike. In Horace 'aequo' (literally 'equal' or 'even') takes on the meaning impartial, ruthless, unremitting.

Eliot's specific literary reference is to the Venetian tragedy *Antonio and Mellida* by John Marston (1575–1634):

> For see the dappled coursers of the morne
> Beat up the light with their bright silver hooves
> And chase it through the sky.   (Pt. II, I, I.)

There is also a local Venetian reference, for the sun's chariot and team is represented on the sculptured bronze doors of the Cathedral of St. Mark.

ll. 11–12: cf. the description of Cleopatra's barge by Enobarbus: 'The barge she sat in, like a burnish'd throne, Burn'd on the water' (*Antony and Cleopatra* II, ii).

l. 18 protozoic: associated with the simplest forms of living matter.

l. 19 Canaletto: Antonio Canale (1697–1768), famous for the many paintings of his favourite subject—the canals of Venice.

l. 21 Rialto: the ancient building in Venice where the principal financial and mercantile business was transacted. 'On the Rialto' is a phrase used by Shylock the Jew in Shakespeare's *Merchant of Venice*, I, iii, with variants of it elsewhere in the play, meaning 'in business quarters'. These associations with Shylock the money-lender are continued in lines 22–3.

l. 24 Money in furs: meaning that there is a fortune to be made in the fur trade, which is a Jewish trade, rather than that the rich dress in furs. Venice was once a centre for the fur trade from the Black Sea.

l. 26 phthisic: consumptive.

l. 27 Lights, lights: cf. 'Light, I say! Light!' the cry of Brabantio in *Othello* I, I. He has just been aroused from sleep by the shouted news that his daughter Desdemona has stolen away to be married to Othello, 'the Moor of Venice', an action that is represented to him as being unnatural and treacherous, a view he accepts.

l. 29 lion's wings: the winged lion was the emblem of the Venetian Republic; and cf. 'Devouring Time, blunt thou the lion's paws', the opening line of Shakespeare's Sonnet I.

ll. 31–2 meditating on/Time's ruins: cf. 'To meditate among decay, and stand/A ruin amidst ruins', *Childe Harold's Pilgrimage* (IV, xxv) by Lord Byron (1788–1824). These lines occur in the stanza that concludes Byron's celebration of Venice, honouring its great past, deploring its present decay, which he sees to be moral, as well as political, financial and architectural.

l. 32 the seven laws: probably a reference to the seven principles of architecture which John Ruskin (1819–1900) set out in *The Seven Lamps of Architecture* (1849), which presents Gothic as the highest style. His study of Gothic art, *The Stones of Venice* (1851–3), relates the greatness and eventual decline of Venetian Gothic to the moral and cultural decline he sees in the Venetian state.

Eliot may also be referring to the Noachian Laws, the 'Seven Commandments of the Sons of Noah' derived from the Talmud, Jewish civil and ceremonial law. The Laws prohibit idolatry, murder, blasphemy, incest, theft, the eating of flesh taken from the limb of a live animal, and require the establishment of courts of law.

SWEENEY ERECT

Probably written 1919; Art and Letters *(London) Summer*
1919

Title: the title neatly points the sexual aspect of the poem's
situation; also the joke on Sweeney as a human animal, human
by scientific definition as an 'erectus', a creature walking up-
right in contrast to the stooping stance of the anthropoid and
higher orders of the ape family. There also seems to be a reference to Ralph Waldo Emerson (1803–82), his essay 'Self-
Reliance' (which also appears to be referred to in lines 25–6).
In the essay's penultimate paragraph Emerson discusses man's
fulfilment: 'He who knows that power is inborn, that he is
weak because he has looked for good out of him and elsewhere,
and, so perceiving, throws himself unhesitatingly on his
thought, instantly rights himself, stands in the erect position,
commands his limbs, works miracles; just as a man who stands
on his feet is stronger than a man who stands on his head.' This
poem effects a grotesque and ironic comment on Emerson's
view.

Eliot said that he thought of Sweeney (who appears in a
number of poems) 'as a man who in younger days was perhaps a pugilist, mildly successful; who then grew older and
retired to keep a pub'. Conrad Aiken, recalling his Harvard
days with Eliot, has suggested that Sweeney is based upon the
ex-pugilist, with a name like Steve O'Donnell, with whom the
poet took boxing lessons at Boston.

Epigraph: from *The Maid's Tragedy* II, ii by Francis Beaumont
(1584–1616) and John Fletcher (1579–1625). The speaker is
the heroine, the broken-hearted Aspatia. Her attendants are at
work on a tapestry which tells the story of Ariadne, in Greek

legend a woman who lost her beloved, as Aspatia has. She criticises their work. The colours are 'not dull and pale enough', and she tells them to take her as their model. The lines quoted in the Epigraph are a continuation of these instructions.

ll. 1–8: these lines echo Aspatia's instructions, particularly her words immediately preceding the Epigraph:

Suppose I stand upon the sea-beach now,
Mine arms thus, and mine hair blown with the wind,
Wild as that desert. . . .

l. 2 Cyclades: a group of islands in the Aegean sea.

l. 3 anfractuous: contorted, craggy.

l. 5 Aeolus: Greek god of the winds.

l. 7 Ariadne: according to Greek legend she was the daughter of Minos, King of Crete. She fell in love with Theseus, and helped him to find his way in and out of the labyrinth, where he killed the Minotaur. They fled from Crete together and were married. But Theseus abandoned her on the island of Naxos where she hanged herself in grief.

l. 8 perjured sails: Theseus had set out from Athens to destroy the Minotaur and so free his country from the annual tribute of young men and women who had to be sent as sacrifices. His success or failure was to be signalled by the colour of the sails of the returning ship. It had set out, with its doomed passengers, bearing black sails; and Theseus forgot to change these on his victorious return journey. His father, the King, saw these and threw himself to his death.

l. 10 Nausicaa: according to Greek legend she was the daughter of King Alcinous on the island of Scheria. She came across Odysseus the morning after he had been ship-wrecked and thrown up on the shore. He was naked, but covered himself with a leafy olive branch and so talked his way into her confidence that she had him brought to the palace under her personal protection. The story is told in Homer's *Odyssey*.

Polypheme: appears in another important 'morning' scene in the *Odyssey*. He was the leader of the Cyclopes, a race of one-eyed man-eating giants. He captured Odysseus and his crew and held them prisoner in his cave. They escaped by blinding him and then hiding into the thick wool on the underside of his flock of sheep, which he let out for their daily pasture.

ll. 25–6: Eliot seems to be referring to two statements in Emerson's essay 'Self-Reliance': 'an institution is the lengthened shadow of one man' and 'all history resolves itself very easily into the biography of a few stout and earnest persons'.

A COOKING EGG

Probably written 1919; Coterie *(London) May 1919*

Title: cooking eggs are usually those which are too old to be eaten on their own, when their staleness might be detected.

Epigraph: 'In the thirtieth year of my life,/When I drank up all my shame.' These are the opening lines of *Le Grand Testament* (*The Great Testament*) by the French poet François Villon (1431–63). He reviews his sins, penitentially, to prepare him to face the after-life; at the same time, he cannot deny his enjoyment of lust and greed.

l. 1 Pipit: perhaps a familiar, affectionate pet-name, or perhaps carrying a learned and obscure 'egg' joke. Pipi is the Greek misrendering of the Hebrew *Yahweh*, regarded by occultists as a word of power: written on a shelled hard-boiled egg, it is said to open the heart to wisdom.

l. 3: presumably a volume of pictures showing the colleges of Oxford University.

l. 5 Daguerreotypes: photographs produced by one of the earliest processes, in use from about 1840–60.

l. 8: probably a piece of sheet music with that title. There are several nineteenth-century songs and piano pieces of that name, the best-known of which is by Weber.

l. 9 I shall not want: cf. 'The Lord is my shepherd; I shall not want' (Psalms xxiii, 1).

l. 10 Sir Philip Sidney: (1554–86), Sidney was the exemplary figure of 'Honour' in Elizabethan England. He was the complete gentleman—courtier, statesman, poet, patron of the arts, and soldier. His humanity is celebrated in the story of his last words, spoken as he lay dying (during an attack on a Spanish convoy) and passed on his cup of water to another wounded man: 'Thy necessity is greater than mine.'

l. 11 Coriolanus: the hero of Shakespeare's *Coriolanus,* a Roman general whom Shakespeare presents as a leader driven by a destructive, selfish 'heroism'.

l. 14 Sir Alfred Mond: (1868–1930), industrial capitalist, founder of Imperial Chemical Industries.

l. 16: financial bonds issued by the British Government, carrying an interest rate of 5 per cent.

l. 18 Lucretia Borgia: (1480–1519), Lucretia was one of the notorious Italian Borgias. Her brother, Cesare, was the poisoner. But Lucretia could undoubtedly provide good 'Society'. She was Duchess of Ferrara, daughter of Cardinal Rodrigo Borgia (afterwards Pope Alexander VI), engaged six times, four times married, and closely associated with the most noble and powerful Italian families.

l. 22 Madame Blavatsky: Helen Petrovna Blavatsky (1831–91), the famous Russian spiritualist and Theosophist, well-known in England and America.

l. 23: the 'Sacred Trances' belong to the secret doctrines of Theosophy, known only to the adepts.

l. 24 Piccarda de Donati: a nun, who was compelled to break her vows. She was consigned by Dante to the lowest level of Heaven, where remain the souls of those who were unable to keep their vows on earth. She addresses Dante (*Paradiso* iii, 25–30) as a child and explains to him the meaning of God's will (70–87).

l. 25 But where; l. 29 Where are: These line openings imitate a classical Latin device, *Ubi sunt* ('Where are') commonly used in poetry to signal sections of regretful recollection. This device is used by Villon in *Le Grand Testament* (see note to Epigraph).

penny world: this name has long been used in the confectionery and baking trades for various kinds of cakes and sweets. Perhaps Eliot is using the words specifically as well as in their wider, metaphorical sense.

l. 26: in some households (particularly in the nineteenth century) it was customary for the children to have some meals with the rest of the family, but at their own table and separated from the adults by a screen. Eliot may be referring to this custom, rather than to some kind of secretive eating.

l. 28: northern suburbs of London.

ll. 29–30: the eagle was one of the emblems of Rome, used particularly by the legions of the army; and these lines probably refer to a Roman force defeated or lost while crossing the Alps of Northern Italy.

l. 33 A.B.C.'s: branches of the Aerated Bread Company's chain of inexpensive restaurants still found throughout London.

THE HIPPOPOTAMUS

Little Review (*Chicago*) *July 1917*

Epigraph: from St. Paul's Epistle to the Colossians iv, 16. This was written in the 1st century A.D. for the benefit of the early Christians at Colossae and Laodicea. Both groups were wavering between Christianity and Judaism. The Epistle is to remind them of their Christian duties and beliefs.

ll. 7–8: the Roman Catholic Church claims direct descent from the ministry of St. Peter to Rome, thus the 'True Church'; 'based upon a rock' recalls the words of Christ to Peter: 'thou art Peter, and upon this rock I will build my church' (Matthew xvi, 18).

l. 23: echoes 'God moves in a mysterious way,/His wonders to perform', the opening lines of 'Light Shining out of Darkness' by William Cowper (1731–1800); and in general Cowper's poem seems to be a point of departure for Eliot's satire.

l. 29: Christ regarded as a sacrificial lamb, whose blood would cleanse man of sin, a metaphorical view of the death of Christ for the salvation of mankind, as in John i, 29: 'Behold the Lamb of God, which taketh away the sin of the world', and Revelation vii, 14, where God's chosen people are described as made 'white in the blood of the lamb' (see line 33).

l. 33: cf. the prayer of the psalmist: 'wash me, and I shall be whiter than snow' (Psalms li, 7), and God's promise that man's 'scarlet' sins 'shall be as white as snow' (Isaiah i, 18).

l. 34 miasmal mist: germ-laden gas from rotting matter.

WHISPERS OF IMMORTALITY

Little Review (*Chicago*) *September 1918*

Title: a play upon 'Intimations of Immortality from Recollections of Early Childhood', an ode by William Wordsworth (1770–1850) concerned with the loss of innocence in experience.

l. 1 Webster: the dramatist John Webster (1580?–1625?) in whose works lust, violence and death are prominent in the plots and poetic imagery.

l. 5: cf. 'A dead man's skull beneath the roots of flowers!' the words of Flamineo in Webster's *The White Devil* v, iv, when Brachiano's ghost enters with a flower-pot of lilies and a skull beneath.

l. 9: the poet John Donne (1572–1631). Eliot's essay 'The Metaphysical Poets' (1921) provides a valuable comment on the entire stanza: 'Tennyson and Browning are poets, and they think, but they do not feel their thought immediately as the odour of a rose. A thought to Donne was an experience; it modified his sensibility.'

l. 20 pneumatic: derived from a Greek word meaning 'spiritual', a joke which is taken up in the next word and in the last four lines of the poem.

l. 29 Abstract Entities: a quasi-philosophical joke, indicating that Grishkin's powers of attraction can compel the attendance even of philosophical terminology. The explanation of these terms would require a philosophical discourse, but something of their meaning can be glimpsed in this quotation from George Berkeley, *Principles of Human Knowledge* (1710): 'The positive abstract idea of quiddity, entity, or existence.'

l. 31 lot: Eliot explained that he is using this word to mean 'kind' (i.e. mankind) not fate.

MR. ELIOT'S SUNDAY MORNING SERVICE

Little Review (*Chicago*) *September 1918*

Epigraph: from *The Jew of Malta* IV, i by Christopher Marlowe (1564–93). These are the words of the servant Ithamore to the Jew, his master Barabas, as he catches sight of two friars. 'Caterpillars' because they exploit their religious office to make a rich living, profiting from their power over the laity. See also note on the Epigraph to 'Portrait of a Lady'.

l. 1: this curiosity is a word of Eliot's invention, meaning (adjectivally) that the 'sutlers' are highly productive of off-spring. But this is not simply an amusing verbal extravagance. The word philoprogenitive occurs in *A New Life of Jesus* by Friedrich Strauss (the English translation 1865, ii, 41) in a discussion of the 'myth' that Jesus was 'begotten' by the Holy Ghost, an area of speculation closely related to the other controversies to which Eliot alludes in this poem.

l. 2 sutlers: provision merchants, usually to an army on the march. These are the bees (of line 25) seen as they pass the church window, their provisioning being the bearing of pollen from flower to flower, a fertilizing activity referred to in line 1. The other 'sapient sutlers' are the learned Christian scholars referred to in lines 31–2, controversialists whose arguments and commentaries on the Bible proliferate, in turn calling into existence further arguments and commentaries, a feature of Church history from the second to the sixth centuries.

l. 4: cf. 'In the beginning was the Word, and the Word was with God, and the Word was God' (John i, 1).

l. 6 Superfetation: a biological term meaning multiple impregnation of an ovary, resulting in twins or larger multiple births.

In the doctrine of Origen (see note to line 8) this would refer to Christ: 'in relation to God this Logos or Son was a copy of the original and, as such, inferior'.

τὸ ἕυ: Greek (to hen), the One.

l. 7 mensual: there is a past-Classical Latin word mensualis, meaning of a month, monthly; presumably, then, this word of Eliot's invention refers to a period of months.

l. 8 Origen: (c. A.D. 185–254), the first and greatest of the early Christian theological scholars, famed for his output of an estimated 6,000 books and enormously long Biblical commentaries. His exegesis of John, chapter one, was particularly elaborate. Hence, one element of meaning in this stanza begins with Eliot's reference to John i, and the offspring of the 'Word' in the many words of Origen and his fellow-commentators. Origen was 'enervate' physically, having castrated himself for the sake of his spiritual health, following Matthew xix, 12: 'there be eunuchs, which have made themselves eunuchs for the kingdom of heaven's sake'. Thus Eliot's reference in line 29 to the 'Blest office of the epicene', in which Origen would be numbered.

A second element of meaning in this stanza relates to particular points in the teachings of Origen: that God is an infinite being, endlessly creating; that Christ was the Word made flesh, the Logos that exists with God from eternity. These views furnished the matter for a number of early heresies, extensively declared and extensively refuted.

Origen was a 'sapient' sutler in supplying the Christian doctrine of the Logos with ideas derived from the concepts of Greek philosophy.

ll. 9–13: Eliot is describing a real or imagined painting of the Baptism of Christ, a favourite subject in Western religious art. The usual treatment of this subject shows Christ standing in a stream or shallow pool, John the Baptist beside him, pouring water over his head from a small bowl. Above Christ's head, the Holy Ghost is often represented by a dove, and over the dove, God looks down from a gap in the clouds. According to the account of the Baptism in Matthew iii, just after the ceremony the Holy Spirit descended and God addressed his Son.

l. 9 Umbrian school: this was a school of painting associated with the area of Umbria in fifteenth-century Italy.

l. 10 gesso: a kind of plaster surface for wall paintings.

l. 16 Paraclete: literally comforter or advocate, a title for the Holy Ghost.

l. 17 presbyters: priests or elders of the Church; Origen was an ordained presbyter.

l. 20 piaculative pence: the collection money, with which the be-pimpled young members of the congregation hope to gain remission for their sins.

ll. 21–4: perhaps another painting, depicting the entrance to Purgatory, through which the souls must pass to be cleansed of sin before they may enter Heaven.

l. 24: cf. 'O for that night! Where I in him/Might live invisible and dim', from 'The Night' by Henry Vaughan (1622–95). Vaughan is a devout soul (line 23) *par excellence.*

ll. 25–8: these lines refer to the 'middleman' function of the bees, carrying the pollen from the stamen (the 'male' organ) of one flower to the pistil (the 'female' seed-bearing part) of another. In this work they can be said to be in contact with both sexes (thus 'epicene'), just as Origen could pass on the word of God to fertilize religious controversies and heresies, and, similarly, as he acted as a go-between, adapting Greek concepts of the Logos for use in Christian theology.

SWEENEY AMONG THE NIGHTINGALES

Written 1918; Little Review (*Chicago*) *September 1918*

Title: perhaps a play upon 'Bianca Among the Nightingales', a poem by Elizabeth Barrett Browning (1806–61). At the end of each stanza there is a reference to singing nightingales, and the poem concludes with associations of hatred and death, echoing the death of Agamemnon (see below):

> They sing for spite,
> They sing for hate, they sing for doom,
> They'll sing through death who sing through night,
> They'll sing and stun me in the tomb—
> The nightingales, the nightingales!

The 'Nightingales' of the title are not only the birds of the final stanzas; the word is also a slang term for prostitutes; and Eliot once remarked to the critic Edmund Wilson that the action of the poem takes place in a dive.

Epigraph: 'Alas, I am struck deep with a mortal blow', the words of King Agamemnon as he is struck down by his wife Clytemnestra in the *Agamemnon* (line 1343) by the Athenian dramatist Aeschylus (525–456 B.C.).

l. 4 maculate: marked, literally, as the giraffe is striped; but this rare word also carries overtones of 'foul' or 'polluted', as we gather from its antonym immaculate, often used to mean virgin, sexually innocent.
l. 5: meteorologically, the appearance of rings round the moon signifies the approach of stormy weather.
l. 6 River Plate: its estuary is on the coast of South America.
l. 7 Raven: a constellation.

64

l. 8 hornèd gate: in classical myth, the gate of horn through which true dreams pass on their way from the underworld to the world of man (see *Aeneid* vi, 892 ff., and *Odyssey* xix, 559 ff.).

l. 9: Orion (the hunter) is a constellation which includes the Dog Star (Sirius). It is one of the brightest in the night sky and so Eliot's 'Gloomy' may be to emphasize that it is clouded over. In the *Aeneid* (i, 535), Vergil refers to 'nimbosus Orion' ('cloudy Orion'), and Eliot may be evoking this classical echo. In the Egyptian calendar, the appearance of Orion forecast the coming of the harvest rain and the Dog Star the approach of the fertilizing Nile floods.

l. 36: a convent of nuns of the Roman Catholic congregation of the Sisters of the Sacred Heart of Jesus and Mary; there were branches of the congregation in South America.

ll. 37–40: Agamemnon was murdered in a bath-house in mid-January, neither the time nor the place for nightingales to be singing. When these anomalies were pointed out to him, Eliot explained that the wood he had in mind was the grove of the Furies at Colonus; he called it 'bloody' because of Agamemnon's murder (which was gruesomely bloody, as he was hacked to death). In *Oedipus at Colonus* by the Athenian dramatist Sophocles (495–06 B.C.), the grove of the Furies is described as filled with singing nightingales.

According to the anthropologist Sir James Frazer, one of the primitive rites to ensure the continuation of the cycles of the seasons was the ritual slaying of the old priest by his successor, an event which took place in the sacred wood, here perhaps echoed in the death of the king within 'the bloody wood'.

Another such reference to vegetation ceremonies described by Frazer may be in lines 19–20, which could be a parody of the harvest offerings to the gods, another ritual to ensure fertility, the quality so markedly absent from the world of Sweeney and his companions. (For Eliot's knowledge of Frazer, see the Prefatory Note to *The Waste Land*, pages 70–1.)

THE WASTE LAND

THE WASTE LAND

Some passages date from before late 1921—Spring 1922, when the body of the poem was assembled; The Criterion *(London) October 1922,* The Dial *(New York) November 1922*

Prefatory Note : The scale and organization of this poem, together with the unusual range of its reference, make it convenient to cover a number of general points in this Prefatory Note, so avoiding the need for lengthy and repetitious explanations in the detailed notes to the poem.

Eliot's immediate Waste Land is the world, as he saw it, after the 1914–18 War. The 'waste' is not, however, that of war's devastation and bloodshed, but the emotional and spiritual sterility of Western man, the 'waste' of our civilization. Eliot does not regard this as a single moment in history, particular to the West in the twentieth century, and the poem is organized to present an inclusive, comparative vision, a perspective of history in which (by succinct allusions and references) twentieth-century forms of belief and disbelief, of culture and of life, are kept in a continuous and critical relationship with those of the past.

The theme of the poem is the salvation of the Waste Land, not as a certainty but a possibility: of emotional, spiritual and intellectual vitality to be regained. Eliot develops this theme drawing upon related patterns in nature, myth and religion: the cycle of the seasons; the ancient fertility myths of Egypt, India and Greece, in which the god must die to be re-born, to bring fertility to the soil and potency to the people; a pattern known to us again in the life, death and resurrection of Christ.

In his notes to the poem, Eliot helpfully refers us to *From Ritual to Romance* (1920) by Jessie Weston (a work based on literary rather than anthropological evidence). He made particular use of her account of the Fisher King, a figure which recurs in a number of fertility myths, and whose story is one of obvious relevance to this poem. His land is under a curse and laid waste. The Fisher King is impotent, by illness or maiming; and his people are likewise infertile. The curse can only be lifted by the arrival of a stranger who must put or answer certain ritual questions.

Eliot relates this myth to the legend of the Grail. The Grail was the cup used by Christ at the Last Supper and in which Joseph of Arimathea caught the blood from the wound made in Christ's side at the Crucifixion, and brought it to Glastonbury in the West of England. The Grail was therefore regarded as a supremely holy Christian relic. It was lost, and the search for the Grail became a powerful narrative image for man's search for spiritual truth, an image used by many medieval writers. The searcher for the Grail is a Knight, whose quest takes him to the Chapel Perilous where he must (like the stranger in the Fisher King myth) put certain questions about the Grail and another holy relic, the Lance which pierced Christ's side. When this is done, the plight of the land and the people is eased.

Eliot also refers to his other major anthropological source, *The Golden Bough* (12 volumes, 1890–1915) by Sir James Frazer, an encyclopaedic study of primitive myth, presenting a possible line of continuity from these origins, through organized religion to modern scientific thought. Clearly, this hypothesis of continuity (as in *From Ritual to Romance*) is of importance to Eliot's interpenetration of past and present in *The Waste Land*. He drew particularly on Frazer's account of the vegetation ceremonies in Part IV, the two volumes treating the deities *Adonis, Attis, Osiris*: these ceremonies were rituals of sacrifice to conciliate the powers of nature and ensure the continuing cycle of the seasons, with the life of the new year to be born again out of the old.

In 1921 Eliot reviewed the ballet of Stravinsky's *Le Sacre du Printemps* (The Rite of Spring), the sequences of which represent primitive vegetation rites. He felt that these ballet sequences were superficial and commented: 'In art there should be interpenetration and metamorphosis. Even *The Golden Bough* can be read in two ways: as a collection of entertaining myths, or as a revelation of that vanished mind of which our mind is a continuum.' These remarks are a clear indication of the way in which Eliot himself read and used Frazer in his poetry.

Epigraph: 'For once I saw with my very own eyes the Sibyl at Cumae hanging in a cage, and when the boys said to her, "Sibyl, what do you want?" she answered, "I want to die." ' These words are spoken by Trimalchio in the *Satyricon*, a satire by the Roman writer Petronius (1st century A.D.). The speaker is drunkenly boasting, trying to surpass his drunken companions in their tales of wonder.

In Greek mythology the Sibyls were women of prophetic powers, that of Cumae the most famous. She was granted long life by Apollo, at her own wish, as many years as she held grains in her hand; but carelessly she forgot to ask for eternal youth. Hence she aged and her prophetic authority declined.

Ezra Pound: (born 1885), the American poet and critic, closely associated with Eliot's work up to the 1920's, and tireless in working to gain recognition for him.

il miglior fabbro: 'the better craftsman' (*Purgatorio* xxvi, 117), Dante's tribute to the twelfth-century poet Arnaut Daniel, emphasizing his superiority over all his Provençal rivals. In 1938 (answering a critic of Pound) Eliot expanded on this tribute: 'the phrase, not only as used by Dante, but as quoted by myself, had a precise meaning. I did not mean to imply that Pound was only that: but I wished at that moment to honour the technical mastery and critical ability manifest in his own work, which had also done so much to turn *The Waste Land* from a jumble of good and bad passages into a poem.' The two poets were in correspondence in 1921–2, Pound setting out detailed advice and suggesting extensive cuts. Eliot recalled in 1946 that the 'sprawling, chaotic poem' left Pound's hands 'reduced to about half its size'. *The Waste Land* was first published without the dedication to Pound. Eliot added these words in January 1923 when he inscribed a presentation copy for his fellow-poet, and they were placed before the poem when *The Waste Land* was reprinted in *Poems 1909–1925*, 1925.

I The Burial of the Dead

Title: 'The Order for The Burial of the Dead' is the full title of the burial service in the Church of England.

ll. 1–18: critics usually contrast this account of April as 'the cruellest month' with the opening to the General Prologue to *The Canterbury Tales* by Chaucer (1343?–1400) which is conventionally energetic and cheerful in accordance with the traditional treatment of Spring. But Eliot may have had a contemporary poem in mind, 'The Old Vicarage, Grantchester' (written and first published 1912, and in *Collected Poems* 1918) by Rupert Brooke (1887–1915). This opens with poignant flashes of memory of his childhood in the English countryside in Springtime, so different from the Berlin scene around him now:

> Just now the lilac is in bloom,
> All before my little room. . . .
> Here am I, sweating, sick, and hot,
> And there the shadowed waters fresh
> Lean up to embrace the naked flesh.
> *Temperamentvoll* German Jews
> Drink beer around . . . .

When the openings to *The Waste Land* and 'Grantchester' are compared it can be seen that there are considerable likenesses in detail and design; and it is likely that Eliot would be expecting the reader to catch the essential dissimilarity between their two views of life, as glimpsed through their accounts of Spring memories and awakenings.

THE WASTE LAND

Eliot's use of *My Past* (1913) by the Countess Marie Larisch, from which come several details in these lines, is discussed in the Introduction, see pages 21-2.

(I should add that in answer to an inquiry Mr. Conrad Aiken told me that although it was possible, in his view, that this section of the poem was written earlier than the rest, he could see no evocation of Rupert Brooke's poetry in *The Waste Land*.)

ll. 2-3: In the mixing of 'memory' and 'desire' Eliot may have been recalling a passage in the opening chapter of *Bubu-de-Montparnasse* (see Introduction, page 18): 'A man walks carrying with him all the properties of his life, and they churn about in his head. Something he sees awakens them, something else excites them. For our flesh has retained all our memories, and we mingle them with our desires.'

ll. 6-7 feeding/A little life: cf. 'Our Mother feedeth thus our little life,/ That we in turn may feed her with our death', from 'To Our Ladies of Death' by James Thomson (1834-82).

l. 8 Starnbergersee: a lake near Munich. Eliot was in Munich in August 1911.

l. 10 Hofgarten: a public park in Munich.

l. 12: 'I am not Russian at all; I come from Lithuania; I am a real German'.

l. 17: In German, there is a romantic and somewhat clichéd expression with precisely this meaning.

l. 20: Eliot's note refers us to Ezekiel ii, 1. God addresses his prophet, 'Son of man, stand upon thy feet, and I will speak unto thee'. Ezekiel is told of his mission, to preach the coming of the Messiah to a rebellious, unbelieving people.

l. 22 broken images: cf. Ezekiel vi, 6, God's judgement upon the people of Israel for worshipping idols: 'and your images shall be broken.'

l. 23: Eliot's note refers us to Ecclesiastes xii, 5, where the preacher describes the desolation of old age: 'Also when they shall be afraid of that which is high, and fears shall be in the way, and the almond tree shall flourish, and the grasshopper shall be a burden, and desire shall fail: because man goeth to his long home, and the mourners go about the streets.'

ll. 25–9: These lines are based upon the opening of one of Eliot's early poems, 'The Death of Saint Narcissus', probably written about 1912:

Come under the shadow of this gray rock—
Come in under the shadow of this gray rock,
And I will show you something different from either
Your shadow sprawling over the sand at daybreak, or
Your shadow leaping behind the fire against the red rock. . . .

'The Death of Narcissus' was set up in type to be printed in *Poetry* (Chicago). A proof was printed, but then suppressed. The poem is now available in *T. S. Eliot, Poems written in early youth* (1967), ed. John Hayward.

l. 25: cf. Isaiah xxxii, 2, describing the blessings of Christ's kingdom: 'And a man shall be as an hiding place from the wind, and a covert from the tempest; as rivers of water in a dry place, as the shadow of a great rock in a weary land.'

l. 30 a handful of dust: This striking phrase is found in Meditation IV of *Devotions Upon Emergent Occasions* (1624) by John Donne: 'what's become of man's great extent and proportion, when himself shrinks himself, and consumes himself to a handful of dust. . . .' The 'fearful' associations, raised in Eliot's line, are Biblical. Dust is the symbolic reminder to man of his bodily mortality, his beginning and end in matter.

Eliot may also be referring obliquely to the Sibyl's fateful request for as many years of life as there are grains of sand in her grasp (see note to the Epigraph, page 71).

ll. 31–4: Eliot's note refers us to the libretto of *Tristan und Isolde* (*Tristan and Isolde*) I, 5–8, the opera by Richard Wagner (1813–83). A sailor is singing about the sweetheart he has left behind him: 'The wind blows fresh to the homeland. My Irish girl, where are you lingering?'

l. 35 hyacinths: these flowers were a symbol for the resurrected god of the fertility rites.

l. 42: Eliot again refers us to Wagner's opera III, 24. Tristan is dying, waiting for Isolde his beloved, but the look-out reports that there is no sign of her ship: 'Desolate and empty the sea.'

l. 43 Madame Sosostris: In the novel *Crome Yellow* (1921) by

74

Aldous Huxley there is a fake fortune-teller, Madame Sesostris (ch. xxvii). Eliot said that he read the novel on its publication in November 1921 and that it is 'almost certain' that he borrowed the name from it, although he was 'unconscious of the borrowing'.

l. 46 pack of cards: this is the Tarot pack, of 78 cards, first known to have been used in France and Italy in the fourteenth century, although many of the symbols and figures are of ancient origin, some of which are said to derive from Egyptian inscriptions, and all of which have been connected with fertility rites and folk lore. The pack is now commonly used in fortune-telling. Eliot notes that he is not familiar with its exact details and that he has departed from them to suit his convenience.

l. 47 Phoenician Sailor: a type of the fertility god, whose image was thrown into the sea each year to symbolize the death of the summer (without which there could be no resurrection, the new year in the spring).

l. 48: a line from the song of Ariel in Shakespeare's *The Tempest* i, ii. Ariel is singing to Ferdinand, telling him of the wonderful 'sea-change' that has taken place for his father, Alonso, King of Naples. In fact, Alonso has not been drowned; Ferdinand thinks he is; and Ariel sings a kind of comforting song, leading him to Miranda, with whom he falls in love.

l. 49 Belladonna: literally, in Italian, beautiful lady; also the popular name for a flower from which is obtained a dangerous drug, used by women to enlarge the pupil of the eye; also the name for one of the three Fates of classical legend (hence, perhaps, line 50).

Lady of the Rocks: the ominous, fateful overtones of the context suggest that Eliot had in mind a passage in *The Renaissance* (1873) where Walter Pater (1839–94) is discussing La Gioconda, more popularly known as the Mona Lisa, the portrait by Leonardo da Vinci of a woman on whose face there is the hint of a strange, haunting smile: 'She is older than the rocks among which she sits; like the vampire, she has been dead many times, and learned the secret of the grave; and had been a diver in deep seas, and keeps their fallen day about her; and trafficked for strange webs with Eastern merchants. . . .'

l. 51 man with three staves: a figure in the Tarot pack. Eliot notes that he associates him, quite arbitrarily, with the Fisher King.

Wheel: the wheel of fortune, figuring the reversals of fortune in life.

ll. 53–4: the Syrian merchants transmitted the mysteries of the Attis cult and the Grail legend.

l. 55 Hanged Man: a figure in the Tarot pack, hanging by one foot from a T-shaped cross. He represents the god killed in order that his resurrection can renew the fertility of the land and its people. Eliot tells us that in his mind the Hanged Man is associated with the Hanged God (sacrificed to ensure fertility) of Frazer, and with the hooded figure mentioned in lines 360–6.

l. 60: Eliot refers us to 'Les Septs Vieillards' ('The Seven Old Men') by Charles Baudelaire (1821–67), quoting 'Fourmillante cité, cité pleine de reves,/Où le spectre en plein jour raccroche le passant' ('Crowded city, city full of dreams,/Where in broad daylight the spectre stops the passer-by'). In 1950 Eliot declared that these two lines summed up Baudelaire's 'significance' for him.

l. 62 London Bridge: a bridge across the Thames; the crowd is of workers on their way to the City district of London, the financial and business area.

ll. 63–4: for the use of Dante in these lines, see Eliot's explanation quoted in the Introduction, page 23.

l. 63: Eliot refers us to Dante, *Inferno* iii, 55–7, quoting 'si lunga tratta/di gente, ch'io non avrei mai creduto,/che morte tanta n'avesse disfatta' ('such a long stream of people, that I should never have believed that death had undone so many'). This is Dante's reaction to seeing the vast crowd of unhappy spirits— those who in life knew neither good or evil, who never learnt to care for anyone but themselves.

l. 64: Eliot refers us to Dante, *Inferno* iv, 25–7, quoting 'Quivi, secondo che per ascoltare,/non avea pianto, ma' che di sospiri,/

che l'aura eterna facevan tremare' ('Here, there was to be heard no sound of lamentation, only sighs which disturbed the eternal air'). Dante is in Limbo. The sighs are those of the people who lived on earth virtuously but unbaptized, before the coming of Christ. Now they exist with the desire but without the hope of seeing God.

l. 66 King William Street: a street in the City of London.

l. 67 Saint Mary Woolnoth: a city church in King William Street. Like the church of Saint Magnus the Martyr, this church was referred to in a report 'Proposed Demolition of 19 City Churches' (1920), mentioned by Eliot in his note to line 264. The Report, submitted to the London County Council by its Clerk and Architect, recommended the preservation of both these churches.

l. 68: Eliot provides a personal note to the effect that he has often noticed the 'dead' (flat) sound in the last stroke of the clock's nine o'clock chimes. But this rather trivial observation may be a derisive joke, a slight distraction from the line's more serious possibilities of meaning. For the City worker in the 1920's 9 a.m. was the usual starting-time for the office day. Beyond this, attending to Eliot's use of the words 'dead' and 'final', some commentators have noted that the death of Christ took place at the ninth hour (this being not 9 a.m. but the ninth hour of daylight, i.e. about 3 p.m.).

l. 69 'Stetson': anyone then in Eliot's circle would have recognized this as referring to Ezra Pound, nicknamed 'Buffalo Bill' for his emphatic Americanism in London; his favourite hat was a sombrero-stetson; *'always* the Westerner in excelsis', said the writer Wyndham Lewis.

l. 70 Mylae: the battle of Mylae (260 B.C.) took place in the first Punic war (a war about trade) between the Romans and the Carthaginians.

l. 71: in ancient fertility rites images of the gods were buried in the fields.

l. 74: Eliot's note refers us to the dirge sung by Cornelia in *The White Devil*, v, iv, by John Webster. She is singing for 'The friendless bodies of unburied men'—'But keep the wolf far thence, that's foe to men,/For with his nails he'll dig them up again.' The change from 'wolf' to 'Dog' is easily made. In the Old Testament, the dog is no 'friend to man', but an unclean animal, living on human corpses. Sometimes the dog is figured as an agent of evil, as in Psalms xxii, 20: 'Deliver my soul from the sword, my darling from the power of the dog.'

l. 76: Eliot refers us to *Fleurs du Mal* (*Flowers of Evil*), a volume of poems by Charles Baudelaire. Eliot's line (after 'You!') is the final line in Baudelaire's prefatory poem, 'Au Lecteur' ('To the Reader'): 'O hypocrite reader, my fellow-man, my brother!'

II A Game of Chess

Title: cf. the title of *A Game at Chess*, a play by Thomas Middleton (1580–1627), who also wrote *Women Beware Women* to which Eliot refers in his note to line 138, specifically to the chess game played there.

l. 77: Eliot refers us to *Antony and Cleopatra* II, ii, the opening of Enobarbus's description of Cleopatra's ceremonial barge and her first meeting with Antony: 'The barge she sat in, like a burnish'd throne,/Burn'd on the water.'

l. 92 laquearia: a panelled ceiling. Eliot refers us to Virgil's *Aeneid* i, 726, quoting 'dependent lychni laquearibus aureis incensi, et noctem flammis funalia vincunt' ('flaming torches hang from the golden-panelled ceiling, and the night is pierced by the flaring lights'). The scene is the banquet given by Dido, Queen of Carthage, in honour of her beloved, Aeneas, who eventually deserts her.

l. 93 coffered: decorated with sunken panels.

l. 98 Sylvan scene: Eliot refers us to Milton's *Paradise Lost* iv, 140. This is the 'scene' before Satan when he first arrives at the borders of Eden.

l. 99: Eliot's note refers us to *Metamorphoses* vi by the Roman poet Ovid (43 B.C.–A.D.18). Ovid's version of the Greek myth tells how Philomela was raped by King Tereus of Thrace (the husband of her sister Procne), how he cut out her tongue, and how she was eventually transformed into a nightingale and so escaped his murderous rage.

l. 103 Jug Jug: in Elizabethan poetry this was a conventional way of representing bird-song; it was also, in contrast, a crude joking reference to sexual intercourse.

l. 118: Eliot refers us to, 'Is the wind in that door still?' from *The Devil's Law Case*, III, ii by John Webster. The remark is made by one surgeon to another when he hears a groan from a man supposed dead. But in 1938 Eliot denied that this source was of any significance; his words, he said, were 'an adaptation of a phrase of Webster which Webster uses with quite a different meaning'. The modern equivalent of Webster's phrase is, 'Is that the way the land lies?' or, 'Is that the way the wind blows?'

l. 125: see note to line 48.

l. 128 Shakespeherian Rag: Rag, short for ragtime, a style of jazz dance music, very popular at the beginning of the First World War. The 'oooo' and the extra syllable in 'Shakespe*he*rian' catch the syncopated rhythm of ragtime music and songs.

l. 137: Eliot's note refers us to the game of chess in Middleton's *Women Beware Women* II, ii. In this scene the mother-in-law's attention is held by a game of chess with Livia, a procuress; every move corresponds to a step in the forceful seduction of Bianca, her daughter-in-law.

l. 139 demobbed: a slang abbreviation of demobilized, meaning released from military service, as conscripted troops were after the First World War.

l. 141: the call of the bartender at closing time in a British public-house.

l. 172: these are Ophelia's last words in *Hamlet* IV, v. She drowns herself, driven mad by Hamlet's pretended affection and then his assumed indifference towards her.

III The Fire Sermon

The Fire Sermon was preached by the Buddha against the fires of lust, anger, envy and the other passions that consume men.

l. 173 river's tent: The immediate, visual image is of the shelter provided in summer by the leafy boughs of the trees overhanging the river, a shelter now broken by the loss of the leaves at the close of the year. But the rhetorical ring of the first half line suggests more solemn overtones of meaning; perhaps the loss is of some sacred or mystic quality. In the Old Testament 'tent' can mean tabernacle or holy place, arising from the use of a tent as a portable tabernacle by the wandering tribes of Israel in the wilderness. In Isaiah xxxiii, 20–1, the 'river' is linked with the 'tent' as an image of the power and security that God offers to his chosen people: 'Look upon Zion, the city of our solemnities: thine eyes shall see Jerusalem a quiet habitation, a tabernacle that shall not be taken down; not one of the stakes thereof shall ever be removed, neither shall any of the cords thereof be broken. But there the glorious Lord will be unto us a place of broad rivers and streams. . . .'

ll. 175–9: for line 176, Eliot refers us to his source, the refrain to 'Prothalamion' by Edmund Spenser (1552–99). The poem is a lyrical celebration of the ideals and joys of marriage written in honour of the double marriage of the daughters of the Earl of Worcester in 1596. The setting is the Thames in a flawless pastoral vision, with the 'Nymphes . . . All lovely Daughters of the Flood' in attendance upon their river, which they strew with flowers to honour this 'Brydale day'.

l. 182: cf. the lamentation of the Israelites recalling their exile in Babylonia and yearning for their homeland, Psalms cxxxvii, 1: 'By the rivers of Babylon, there we sat down, yea, we wept, when we remembered Zion.' 'the waters of Leman' is a phrase associated with the fires of lust, from the meaning of leman as mistress or prostitute.

Lake Leman is the French name for Lake of Geneva in

Switzerland; in the nearby town of Lausanne, early in 1922, Eliot continued the writing of *The Waste Land*, on which he had been working at Margate three or four months earlier (see note to l. 300).

l. 185: cf. 'But at my back I always hear/Time's winged chariot hurrying near', from 'To His Coy Mistress' by Andrew Marvell (see 'Prufrock', note to line 23).

l. 192: Eliot refers to *The Tempest* I, ii, where Ferdinand is thinking of his father (see note to line 48), reminded by Ariel's music: 'Sitting on a bank,/Weeping again the king my father's wrack.'

l. 193: continuing the ritual referred to in the note to line 47, the image was taken out of the water to symbolize the god's resurrection.

l. 196: Eliot refers us to 'To His Coy Mistress', see note to line 185.

l. 197: Eliot refers us to *The Parliament of Bees*, a play by John Day (1574–1640?), quoting:

> When of a sudden, listening, you shall hear,
> A noise of horns and hunting, which shall bring
> Actaeon to Diana in the Spring,
> Where all shall see her naked skin.

According to the Greek legend, the huntsman Actaeon surprised Diana (goddess of chastity) bathing with her nymphs. As a punishment he was turned into a stag and hunted to death.

ll. 199–201: Eliot notes that these lines come from a ballad popular among Australian troops in the First World War; notably, it was sung as they landed in Gallipoli in 1915. It was reported to him from Sydney, Australia. There are several versions. Possibly Eliot heard a polite version, which misses the point that Mrs. Porter was a legendary brothel-keeper in Cairo:

> O the moon shines bright on Mrs. Porter
> And on the daughter of Mrs. Porter.

And they both wash their feet in soda water
And so they oughter
To keep them clean.

Years later, Eliot emphasized that the soda water is not the aerated drink but bicarbonate of soda solution. Concerning Mrs. Porter and her daughter, Eliot told Clive Bell that 'These characters are known only from an Ayrian camp-fire song of which one other line has been preserved: *And so they oughter*. Of such pieces, epic or didactic, most have been lost, wholly or in part, in the mists of antiquity. . . .'

l. 202: Eliot refers us to his source, the final line to the sonnet 'Parsifal' by Paul Verlaine (1844–96): 'And, O those children's voices singing in the dome.' Verlaine is referring to Wagner's *Parsifal* and its music. In the Grail Legend, the choir of children sings at the ceremony of the foot-washing which precedes the restoration of the wounded Anfortas (the Fisher King) by the Knight Parzival and the lifting of the curse from the waste land.

l. 204: see note to line 103.

l. 205: a phrase from *A Game at Chess* (see note to Title, Section II).

l. 206: Tereu (the Latin vocative form of Tereus) refers to King Tereus, who raped (line 205) Philomela (see note to line 99). This interpretation of the bird's song is found in Trico's song *Alexander and Campaspe* by John Lyly (1554–1606?): 'Oh, 'tis the ravished nightingale./*Jug, jug, jug, jug, tereu!* she cries'.

l. 209 Smyrna: modern Izmir, in Western Turkey, formerly one of the great trading ports of Asia Minor; between 1919–22, Smyrna was much in the news on account of the rival claims to its possession by Turkey and Greece.

ll. 209–14: The events described here actually happened. Years later Eliot told an inquirer that he had in fact received such an invitation from an unshaven man from Smyrna with currants in his pocket. The homosexual implications that some interpreters have read into these lines did not, said Eliot, occur to him.

l. 211: Eliot explains these commercial terms: c.i.f. is the price inclusive of 'cost, insurance, freight to London'. The second part of the line means that the documents of ownership and transport would be handed to the purchaser in exchange for a bank draft payable on sight.

l. 213 Cannon Street Hotel: a hotel attached to Cannon Street station in the City of London, which was then the main terminus for businessmen travelling to and from the Continent.

l. 214 Metropole: a fashionable luxury hotel at Brighton, on the South Coast of England, sixty miles from London. A 'weekend at Brighton' is understood colloquially as an invitation carrying sexual implications.

ll. 215–23: these lines seem to be modelled upon the evening scene at the opening to the *Purgatorio* viii: 'It was now the hour that turns back the desire of those who sail the seas and melts their heart, that day when they have said farewell to their dear friends, and that pierces the new pilgrim with love, if from far off he hears the chimes which seem to mourn for the dying day' (1–6).

ll. 218–20: in these lines Eliot refers to the prophetic powers and bi-sexuality of Tiresias, quoting the Latin text of Ovid's *Metamorphoses* which tells this legend: Tiresias came across two snakes copulating in a forest. He hit them with his staff and was turned into a woman. Seven years later he saw the same two snakes and hit them again. As he had hoped, he was turned back into a man. On account of Tiresias's male and female experience, Jove called him in as an expert witness to settle a quarrel with his wife Juno. Jove was arguing that in love the woman enjoys the greater pleasure; Juno argued that it was the other way round. Tiresias supported Jove. Out of spite Juno blinded him. To make up for this, Jove gave him the power of prophecy, and long life.

Eliot also draws our attention to the fluidity of the point-of-view in *The Waste Land:* 'Tiresias, although a mere spectator and not indeed a "character", is yet the most important personage in the poem, uniting all the rest. Just as the one-eyed merchant, seller of currants, melts into the Phoenician Sailor, and the latter is not wholly distinct from Ferdinand Prince of Naples, so all the women are one woman, and the two sexes meet in Tiresias. What Tiresias *sees*, in fact, is the substance of the poem.' Curiously, Eliot once signed himself 'Tiresias' in a letter to the Italian scholar Mario Praz.

l. 221: Eliot refers us to Fragment 149 by the Greek poetess Sappho (seventh century B.C.), a prayer to the Evening Star: 'Evening Star, that brings back all that the shining Dawn has sent far and wide, you bring back the sheep, the goat, and the child back to the mother.'

l. 231: Eliot told an enquirer that he intended the phrasing of 'the young man carbuncular' to echo 'that old man eloquent' in Milton's sonnet 'To the Lady Margaret Ley'.

l. 234 Bradford: a manufacturing town in northern England, reputed to have produced a crop of millionaires, men who made their fortunes in supplying woollen goods during the First World War.

ll. 243–5: Eliot is referring to bi-sexual Tiresias (see note to lines 218–200) and to the story of Tiresias in *Oedipus Tyrannus* (*King Oedipus*) by Sophocles (495–406 B.C.). Tiresias, the blind seer, recognizes that the curse on Thebes has been called down by the unknowingly incestuous marriage between Oedipus and his mother Jocasta and Oedipus's killing (again, unknowingly) of his father. Thebes has been turned into a waste land, the people and the land infertile.

l. 246: this probably refers to Homer's account of Tiresias in Hades, where he is consulted by Odysseus (*Odyssey* ii).

l. 253: Eliot refers us to his source, the song of Olivia in *The Vicar of Wakefield*, the novel by Oliver Goldsmith (1730–74). Returning to the spot where she was seduced, she sings this song: 'When lovely woman stoops to folly/And finds too late that men betray/What charm can soothe her melancholy,/What art can wash her guilt away?/The only art her guilt to cover,/To hide her shame from every eye,/To give repentance to her lover/And wring his bosom—is to die.'

l. 257: Eliot refers us to *The Tempest* i, ii, the words of Ferdinand, remembering the music that calmed both the storm at sea and his own storm of grief for his father's supposed death (see note to line 192).

l. 258 Strand: a London street, leading eastwards towards the City of London.

Queen Victoria Street: in the City of London, close to the River Thames.

l. 260 Lower Thames Street: near the river at London Bridge.

ll. 263–5: the city church of St. Magnus Martyr, designed by Sir Christopher Wren.

l. 263 fishmen: workers from nearby Billingsgate fish market, not fishermen.

l. 266: Eliot notes that The Song of the (three) Thames-daughters begins here. The Nymphes in Spenser's 'Prothalamion' are called 'Daughters of the Flood' (see note to lines 175–9).

ll. 266–78: the river is the River Thames at London. Some details of this scene are based upon the description of the river at the opening to 'Heart of Darkness' (1899), a story by Joseph Conrad (1857–1924): 'the tanned sails of the barges drifting up with the tide seemed to stand still in red clusters of canvas'.

The epigraph Eliot chose first for *The Waste Land* was 'The horror! The horror!' from the centre of Conrad's story, a fuller account of which is given in the notes to 'The Hollow Men' (see pages 100–1).

l. 275 Greenwich reach: the south bank of the River Thames at Greenwich, downstream from the centre of London.

l. 276 Isle of Dogs: the river bank opposite Greenwich.

ll. 277–8: the lament of the Rhine-maidens (see note to lines 292–303).

l. 279: Eliot refers us to the *History of England* vii, 349, by J. A. Froude, which quotes a letter, dated 30th June 1561, from Alvarez de Quadra (Bishop of Aquila) to King Philip of Spain, whose Ambassador he was to the English court. De Quadra is reporting his observation of Queen Elizabeth and Lord Robert Dudley, the Earl of Leicester, whom he reported to be Elizabeth's lover: 'In the afternoon we were in a barge, watching the games on the river. She was alone with the Lord Robert and myself on the poop, when they began to talk nonsense and went so far that Lord Robert at last said, as I was on the spot there was no reason why they should not be married if the Queen pleased.' The river is the Thames and Elizabeth entertained Leicester at Greenwich House, near Greenwich reach (see l. 275).

l. 289: probably the ancillary white stone towers of the Tower of London.

ll. 292–303: Eliot notes that the Thames-daughters here speak in turn, and he refers us to Wagner's opera *Die Götterdämmerung* (*The Twilight of the Gods*) III, i. The beauty of the Rhine has been lost with the theft of the river's gold, but the Rhine-maidens are anticipating its immediate return. As in the Grail Legend, the violation has brought down a curse.

l. 293 Highbury: a residential suburb in North London. *Richmond, Kew:* two riverside districts, on the Thames west of London. Eliot refers us to Dante, *Purgatorio* V, 133, quoting 'ricorditi di me, che son la Pia; / Siena mi fe', disfecemi Maremma' ('Remember me, who am La Pia; Siena made me, Maremma unmade me'). La Pia, the Lady of Siena (a town in central Italy), is addressing Dante in Purgatory, where she is among those who failed to repent their sins before death. She is said to have been murdered at Maremma, pushed out of a castle window on her husband's orders.

l. 296 Moorgate: an area in the east of the City of London. Eliot used Moorgate underground railway station when he was working at Lloyds Bank.

l. 300 Margate Sands: a seaside resort on the Thames estuary, popular with Londoners. Here Eliot began *The Waste Land* late in 1921, convalescing from an illness.

l. 307: Eliot refers us to his source, the *Confessions* (iii,1) of St. Augustine (345–430): 'to Carthage then I came, where a cauldron of unholy loves sang all about mine ears'. St. Augustine is here writing of the sensual temptations by which he was assailed in his youth.

l. 308: Eliot refers us to his source, the Fire Sermon of the

Buddha, which Eliot sees to have an importance corresponding to that of Christ's Sermon on the Mount, in which he explained to the people the nature of the Kingdom of Heaven (see Matthew v-vii).

In the Fire Sermon the Buddha tells his followers that everything is on fire: 'forms are on fire . . . impressions received by the eye are on fire; and whatever sensation, pleasant, unpleasant, or indifferent, originates in dependence on impressions received by the eye, that also is on fire. And with what are these on fire? With the fire of passion, say I, with the fire of hatred, with the fire of infatuation. . . .'

l. 309: Eliot refers us to his source, the *Confessions* of St. Augustine: 'I entangle my steps with these outward beauties, but Thou pluckest me out, O Lord, Thou pluckest me out!' Eliot remarks on his purposeful use of the Buddha and the Christian saint, 'representatives of eastern and western asceticism', as the 'culmination' of this section of the poem.

The significance of St. Augustine's words is brought out in God's challenge to Satan: 'is not this a brand plucked out of the fire?' (Zechariah iii, 2). The 'brand' is the High Priest Joshua, once a non-believer, now a follower of the Messiah.

IV Death by Water

According to Jessie Weston, each year at Alexandria an effigy of the head of the god was thrown into the sea as a symbol of the death of the powers of nature. The head was carried by the current to Byblos. It was then retrieved and worshipped as a symbol of the god reborn. Another powerful tradition of a life-bringing death-by-water is contained in the Christian sacrament of Baptism: 'So many of us as were baptized into Jesus Christ were baptized into his death. Therefore we are baptized with him by baptism into death' (Romans vi, 3-4).

This section is a close adaptation of the last seven lines of a French poem by Eliot, 'Dans le Restaurant', written 1916-17:

Phlebas, le Phénicien, pendant quinze jours noyé,
Oubliait les cris des mouettes et la houle de Cornouaille,
Et les profits et les pertes, et la cargaison d'étain:
Un courant de sous-mer l'emporta très loin,
Le repassant aux étapes de sa vie antérieure.
Figurez-vous donc, c'était un sort pénible;
Cependant, ce fut jadis un bel homme, de haute taille.

(Phlebas the Phoenician, a fortnight drowned, forgot the cry of gulls and the swell of the Cornish seas, and the profit and the loss, and the cargo of tin. An undersea current carried him far, took him back through the ages of his past. Imagine it—a terrible end for a man once so handsome and tall.)

l. 312: 'Dans le Restaurant' in turn may have been suggested to Eliot by a passage in the *Life and Death of Jason* (1867) by William Morris (1834–96). In Book IV, the song of Orpheus to the Argonauts refers to a Phoenician sailor as a victim of the sea. At this time Eliot was familiar with the poem and quoted from Book IV in his essay 'Andrew Marvell' (1921).

ll. 315–16: these lines take up the image of 'sea-change' in Ariel's song in *The Tempest* (see note to line 48).

l. 319: i.e. all mankind. The Biblical distinction is between the faithful believers, the Jews, and those who rejected God (see Romans i, 18–32).

V   What the Thunder Said

Title: see note to lines 399–401.

Eliot notes that in the first part, lines 322–94, three themes are employed. First, the story told in Luke xxiv, 13–31 of the two disciples travelling on the road to Emmaus (a village some distance from Jerusalem) on the day of Christ's resurrection. He joins them but remains unrecognized until he blesses their evening meal. Meanwhile, the disciples talk over the recent events—the trial, the crucifixion and so on—referred to in more detail in the notes to lines 322–65.

The second theme specified by Eliot is the approach to the Chapel Perilous. This is the final stage of the Grail quest. The Knight is tested by the illusion of nothingness. This theme is interwoven with the Emmaus story from lines 331–94.

The third theme is the decay of Eastern Europe in the modern world, referred to in detail in the notes to lines 366–76.

ll. 322–8: these lines refer to the course of events from the betrayal and arrest of Christ, after the night of agonized prayer in the garden of Gethsemane, until the moment of his death.

l. 322: John xviii reports the arrest of Christ in the garden of Gethsemane: Judas, the chief priests and 'a band of men and officers . . . cometh thither with lanterns and torches and weapons'.

l. 326: Christ was taken under arrest to the palace of the High Priest where he was publicly interrogated, before being taken to Pilate, the Roman Governor, in the Hall of Judgement.

l. 327: at the death of Christ the earth shook (see Matthew xxvii, 51).

l. 346 If . . . rock: This is printed as two lines, but the line numbering of the text, followed in these notes, counts the words as a single line.

ll. 360–5: Eliot notes that these lines were stimulated by the account (in *South,* 1919, by Sir Ernest Shackleton) of an Antarctic expedition on which the exhausted explorers were haunted by the delusion that there was one more person with them than could be counted.

ll. 368–9: Eliot refers us to *Blick ins Chaos* (1920) (*A Glimpse into Chaos*) by Hermann Hesse (1872–1962), and quotes a passage from the German text, referring to the Russian Revolution and other upheavals in Europe: 'Already half of Europe, already at least half of Eastern Europe, on the way to Chaos, drives drunkenly in spiritual frenzy along the edge of the abyss, sings drunkenly, as though singing hymns, as Dmitri Karamazov [in *The Brothers Karamazov* by the Russian novelist Feodor Dostoevsky (1821–81)] sang. The offended bourgeois laughs at the songs; the saint and the seer hear them with tears.'

ll. 371–6: When he read these lines, the philosopher Bertrand Russell recalled that he had once told Eliot of a nightmare in which he had a vision of London as an unreal city, its inhabitants like hallucinations, its bridges collapsing, its buildings passing into a mist.

l. 377: the hair was both a symbol of fertility and an object of sacrifice to the fertility gods.

ll. 379–84: Medieval versions of the Grail Legend tell of the horrors with which the Chapel Perilous was filled to test the Knight's courage, and of the nightmare visions, including bats with baby faces, that assail him on his approach. According to Eliot some of the details here were inspired by a painting of the school of Hieronymus Bosch, the fifteenth-century Dutch artist. Some of his best known works are mysterious, often grotesque and horrifying visions of Hell, its devils, temptations and torments.

ll. 382–3: the church bells of London (cf. line 67); and according to Jessie Weston a bell was rung at the Chapel Perilous to signify that the knight has survived his ordeal.

l. 384: in the language of the Old Testament the empty wells and cisterns would signify the drying up of faith and the worship of false gods, cf. the words of God to his prophet Jeremiah: 'For my people have committed two evils; they have forsaken me the fountain of living waters, and carved themselves out cisterns, broken cisterns that can hold no water' (Jeremiah ii, 13); and the words of Solomon to his people: 'Drink waters out of thine own cistern, and running waters out of thine own well' (Proverbs v, 15).

ll. 391–2: Eliot may be drawing upon two traditions of the crowing cock. Firstly, the story told in the Gospels: that as Christ foretold, his disciple Peter denied acquaintance with him when Christ was under arrest before his trial; this happened three times, and when a cock had crowed twice, Peter broke down in tears at his own shame and cowardice. In this context, the crowing of the cock is seen as part of the ritual preceding the death of Christ, salvation for mankind.

The second tradition is that of the cock as 'trumpet of the morn', a signal to ghosts and spirits that as darkness fades they must return to their homes, as the Ghost of Hamlet's father disappears at its call in *Hamlet* I, i. The chapel is now empty of nightmares and apparitions.

l. 395 Ganga: the sacred Indian River Ganges.

l. 397 Himavant: a holy mountain in the Himalaya range.

ll. 399–401: Eliot refers us to the source of the Indian legend of the Thunder in the sacred book *Brihadaranyaka-Upanishad* v, 1. Three groups—gods, demons, men—approach the creator Parajapti and each in turn asks him to speak. To each group he answers 'DA'. Each group interprets this reply differently (in lines 401, 411, 418). According to the fable, 'This is what the divine voice, the Thunder, repeats when he says DA, DA, DA: "Control yourselves; give alms; be compassionate." '

l. 401 Datta: Sanskrit for give. Eliot studied this language at Harvard 1911–13. It is used again in lines 411, 418, 432.

l. 407: Eliot refers us to *The White Devil*, v, vi, by John Webster, the speech of Flamineo warning against the inconstancy of women:

> . . . they'll re-marry
> Ere the worm pierce your winding-sheet, ere the spider
> Make a thin curtain for your epitaphs.

l. 411 Dayadhvam: sympathize.

Eliot refers us to Dante, *Inferno* xxxiii, 46, quoting the words of Ugolino della Gherardesca, a thirteenth-century Italian noble, as he recalls his imprisonment in a tower with his two sons and two grandsons, where they starved to death: 'ed io sentii chiavar l'uscio di sotto/all'orribile torre' ('and below I heard the door of the horrible tower being locked up'). Ugolino heard the key 'turn once only,' for when the prisoners were inside and the door locked, the key was thrown into a river and the prisoners left to starve.

Eliot also quotes from *Appearance and Reality* (1893) by the philosopher F. H. Bradley (1846–1924): 'My eternal sensations are no less private to myself than are my thoughts or feelings. In either case my experience falls within my own circle, a circle closed on the outside; and, with all its elements alike, every sphere is opaque to the others which surround it. . . . In brief, regarded as an existence which appears in a soul, the whole world for each is peculiar and private to that soul.' Eliot was a close student of Bradley. His Harvard doctoral thesis (begun October 1911, completed April 1916) was entitled 'Knowledge and Experience in the Philosophy of F. H. Bradley' and was published under this name in 1964.

l. 416 Coriolanus: the title-hero of Shakespeare's play, 'broken' because pride and selfish integrity brought about his death to the shouts of the mob he despised.

ll. 418–22: When young, Eliot was a keen yachtsman.

l. 423–4: Eliot refers us to the chapter on the Fisher King in *From Ritual to Romance.*

l. 425: cf. the words of the prophet Isaiah to King Hezekiah, a sick man whose kingdom lies waste under Assyrian conquest: 'Thus saith the Lord, Set thine house in order: for thou shalt die, and not live' (Isaiah xxxviii, 1). Hezekiah prays for mercy and God answers him, promising to deliver his country from the Assyrians and granting him a further fifteen years of life.

Compare also, 'Set my love in order, O thou who lovest me' ('Ordina quest' amore, O tu che m' ami'), a prayer of the Italian poet Jacopone da Todi (1230–1306), placed by Dante at the head of the *Purgatorio.*

l. 426: 'London Bridge is falling down, falling down,/London Bridge is falling down,/My fair lady', the refrain of a nursery rhyme.

l. 427: Eliot refers us to his source in Dante, *Purgatorio* xxvi, 145–8: ' "Ara vos prec, per aquella valor/que vos guida al som de l'escalina,/sovegna vos a temps de ma dolor."/Poi s'ascose nel foco che gli affina' ("And so I pray you, by that virtue which leads you to the topmost of the stair—be mindful in due time of my pain." Then dived he back into that fire which refines them.') As he climbs the Mount of Purgatory, Dante is addressed by Arnaut Daniel, speaking here in his native Provençal, now suffering the punishment of the lustful in the cleansing fires of Purgatory. Eliot commented on these lines: 'The souls in purgatory suffer because they wish to suffer, for purgation . . . in their suffering is hope' ('Dante').

l. 428 Quando . . . chelidon: 'When shall I be like the swallow?' a line which Eliot refers to its source in an anonymous Latin poem, 'Pervigilium Veneris' ('The Vigil of Venus'). The poet laments that his song is unheard and asks when the Spring will return to give it voice, like the swallow. Eliot also refers to the story of Procne (see note to line 99), touched upon at the close of the hymn, who was turned into a swallow.

l. 429: 'The Prince of Aquitaine, of the ruined tower', a line which Eliot refers to its source in the sonnet 'El Desdichado' ('The Disinherited') by Gerard de Nerval (1808–55). The poet refers to himself as the disinherited Prince, heir to the tradition of the French troubadour poets who were associated with the castles of Aquitaine in Southern France. One of the cards in the Tarot pack is the tower struck by lightning, symbolizing a lost tradition.

l. 431: Eliot refers us to his source in *The Spanish Tragedy* by Thomas Kyd (1557?–95), sub-titled *Hieronymo is Mad Againe.* Hieronymo is driven mad by the murder of his son. Asked to write a court entertainment he replies, 'Why then Ile fit you!' a double-edged agreement, for he arranges that his son's murderers are themselves killed in his little play, which was made up from fragments of poetry in 'sundry languages' (exactly as here in *The Waste Land*).

l. 432: Give. Sympathize. Control.

l. 433: Eliot's note tells us that this Sanskrit word so repeated signifies 'The peace which passeth understanding', and serves as the formal ending to the Upanishads, the poetic dialogues and commentary which follow the Vedas, the ancient Hindu scriptures. Eliot's interpretation derives from the words of Paul to the early Christians: 'And the peace of God, which passeth all understanding, shall keep your hearts and minds through Christ Jesus' (Philippians iv, 7).

THE HOLLOW MEN

THE HOLLOW MEN

For details of composition and publication (1925) see Appendix

Prefatory Note: 'The Hollow Men' is an extraordinarily difficult poem to annotate. Its language and imagery are disarmingly simple. There are no problems of historical reference or translation. But it is highly allusive, allusive almost to the point of obscurity, and the identification of Eliot's sources cannot be made without some degree of interpretation. My method has been to consider one-by-one the four major sources or areas of reference, and then to provide an item-by-item identification and interpretative commentary in the detailed notes to the poem.

The four major sources or areas of reference are the historical account of the Gunpowder Plot; the assassination of Caesar as presented in Shakespeare's *Julius Caesar*; Conrad's story, 'Heart of Darkness' (see *The Waste Land*, note to lines 266–78); and the three parts of Dante's *Divina Commedia*.

Eliot's use of the first two sources is straightforward, and particular points of reference are detailed in the notes to the poem. At this stage, however, it may be useful for some readers to have the general facts before them.

(i) *The Gunpowder Plot:* In the Epigraph, Eliot refers to the present-day celebration of the plot's failure; and he closes the poem with another, more tragic allusion.

The plot had its origin in the resentment of the English Catholics under James I. After the death of Elizabeth, they had hoped for a more liberal régime. But, instead, they found themselves under the threat of suppression. A group of extremist Catholics was brought together by Robert Catesby, a brave man wit a hdominating personality. Their plan was to seize power by killing King James and all his ministers at the State Opening of Parliament, thus leaving the country without a King and government.

But Francis Tresham, one of the conspirators, inadvertently betrayed the plot when he wrote to his brother-in-law, Lord Monteagle, warning him to keep away from the Houses of Parliament on the day of the State Opening, 5th November 1605. Monteagle informed the Lord Chancellor of this warning, and in turn the King was told. Catesby got wind of this but decided nevertheless to attempt the mass-assassination. Thus, on the night of 4th November, Guy Fawkes was arrested in the cellars of the House of Lords where he stood guard over nearly two tons of gunpowder. After days of torture he broke down and revealed the names of the other conspirators. Those who had not fled the country were executed.

The circumstances of the plot seem to be referred to in line 10 ('dry cellar'), line 16 ('violent souls'), and in the operation of the Shadow in section five, whatever it is in human affairs or within human beings that prevents fulfilment and success. The failure of the plot sounds clearly in the final lines, a macabre-comic chorus. Indeed the world of the King, his Lords and his Commons did not end with an explosive 'bang' that day, whereas for Guy Fawkes and his fellow-conspirators there was the 'whimper' of death.

(*ii*) *Julius Caesar:* This, like the Gunpowder Plot, is a conspiracy of men who resort to violence and who are blinded by their cause. Shakespeare's play is alluded to indirectly in the poem's title and specifically in lines 72 to 90 (Brutus's soliloquy is quoted fully in the notes). Brutus, a leading Roman citizen, is approached by Cassius who is gathering a group to assassinate Julius Caesar, the head of the Roman state. Cassius is motivated by ambition, envy and personal malice. But he persuades Brutus that Caesar is himself an ambitious tyrant who will destroy the tradition of Roman republicanism.

Cassius plays upon Brutus's vanity, his self-importance as the head of a leading Roman family, famed for its championing of the public good, and upon his sense of personal honour, which blinds him to the possibility that the plot is evil. In terms of the dramatic action, Brutus, the man who would lay claim to the highest motives, is shown up as the hollowest of them all, the most deceived and self-deceiving.

(*iii*) Eliot's use of Dante is more indirect and much more important. The three books of the *Divina Commedia* compose an allegorical dream-vision in which Dante himself is conducted through the Hell of punishment and of lost souls (in the *Inferno*), the Purgatory of suffering towards redemption (*Purgatorio*), and Paradise, a higher, perfect world of beauty, light and music (*Paradiso*). Putting the matter very arbitrarily, it can be said that the condition of the hollow men is that of the lost souls in Hell. They are the inhabitants of 'death's dream kingdom' gathered at their last meeting-place beside a 'tumid river' (lines 57–60). In Dante, this corresponds to the scene beside the River Acheron (*Inferno* iii) where the spirits of the damned wait to be ferried across to Hell. There is also another group, which seems to correspond more precisely to Eliot's hollow men. These are the shades which have never been spiritually alive, never experienced good or evil, having lived narrowly for themselves. They are rejected by both Heaven and Hell, and are condemned to stay eternally by the river. Eliot seems to be referring to their condition in lines 11–12. In *The Waste Land* (see note to line 63) Eliot associated them with the crowds crossing London Bridge. In this respect, the hollow men are not narrowly the conspirators; they are all mankind (an interpretation supported by Eliot's use of 'Heart of Darkness').

Eliot refers to a second kingdom, 'death's other kingdom'. If 'death's dream kingdom' is related to the fallen, sinful world of the *Inferno* and *Purgatorio*, this second kingdom is related to the *Paradiso*, and the aspect of this perfect world which Dante glimpses in the closing books of the *Purgatorio*. Here we read of Dante's arrival at the summit of the Mount of Purgatory, at the top of which is the Earthly Paradise, the Garden of Eden where he meets Beatrice, formerly his beloved on earth, now a figure of blessedness, spiritual beauty, and revelation. Section

II of Eliot's poem is concerned with the courage and self-scrutiny which needed even to catch a glimpse of that vision.

There is a third kingdom, 'death's twilight kingdom' (lines 38, 65). This seems to be a transitional stage between the 'dream' and the 'other' kingdoms. In Dante, it corresponds with the poet's progress towards Beatrice in the Earthly Paradise. He has first to pass through the River Lethe, which flows in shadow, then through the River Eumoë: the first river washes away all memory of sin, the second restores the memory of righteousness. It is a stage at which Dante is humbled and shamed by the memory of his sins and unfaithfulness to Beatrice. In the scheme of Eliot's poem, this 'twilight kingdom' is the condition in which man has to face the truth about himself and life, as Kurtz does (see note iv, below). The fourth kingdom is the kingdom of God, which can be spoken of only in broken words (see line 77).

(*iv*) It is quite impossible to convey in summary notes the complexity of the relationship between 'The Hollow Men' and 'Heart of Darkness'. Next to Dante, Conrad's story is arguably the most important single literary experience in Eliot's poetry from 'Prufrock' onwards. He once described it as an outstanding instance of the literary evocation of evil. Conrad's story is full of hollow men—empty of faith, of personality, of moral strength, of humanity. Marlow tells of his journey into a nightmare kingdom of death, the heart of darkness in the forests of the Congo, where he feels himself to have 'stepped into the gloomy circle of some Inferno' and sees around him figures 'in all the attitudes of pain, abandonment, and despair' (a scene which could come straight from Dante). There is a constant and emphatic imagery of eyes (matched in Eliot) of whispers, of shades and shadows, of twilight greyness, of formlessness and impalpability, of inertia, paralysis, unfulfilment and aimlessness. In a native village beside a river, an 'infernal stream', at the heart of the jungle Marlow comes to Kurtz, 'the hollow sham', the man who came from Europe full of an empty, rhetorical idealism, which collapsed under the force of the savage, barbaric 'darkness'.

THE HOLLOW MEN

Conrad's affirmation is that all men are hollow, all fated to endure the condition that Eliot figures so allusively in 'The Hollow Men', and all fated to be blind to their condition; all, excepting those few, and Kurtz himself is one, who are able, eventually, to glimpse and face this horrifying truth. This is the force of Eliot's 'We' in the opening lines; it is the 'We' of all mankind, save for 'Those who have crossed/With direct eyes' (lines 13–14) like Kurtz, whose dying 'stare' remains to haunt Marlow: 'his stare . . . wide enough to embrace the whole universe, piercing enough to penetrate all the hearts that beat in the darkness . . . that wide and immense stare embracing, condemning, loathing all the universe'. This is the stare with which Kurtz meets the vision of ultimate truth, in a 'supreme moment of complete knowledge', greeting it with his final cry —'The horror! The horror!', the words that signified so much to Eliot that he planned to use them as the Epigraph to *The Waste Land*.

Epigraph to section in 'Selected Poems': the words are spoken by a servant in 'Heart of Darkness', reporting Kurtz's death.

Title: In answer to a scholarly suggestion Eliot explained in 1935 that he had made up this title by combining that of 'The Hollow Land', a romance by William Morris (1834–96) with 'The Broken Man', a poem by Rudyard Kipling (1865–1936).

The phrase 'hollow men' occurs in *Julius Caesar* IV, ii, where it is used by Brutus when he learns that his former ally and fellow-conspirator Cassius is now behaving in a less friendly way towards him. Brutus reflects:

> But hollow men, like horses hot at hand,
> Make gallant show and promise of their mettle;
> But when they should endure the bloody spur,
> They fail their crests, and, like deceitful jades,
> Sink in the trial.

'Heart of Darkness' also contributes to the poem's title.

THE HOLLOW MEN

Kurtz is described as a 'hollow sham', and the theme of hollow-ness runs through the story.

Epigraph to poem: a version of the children's cry—'A penny for the Guy!'—when begging money to buy fireworks for the celebration of Guy Fawkes Day. The Guy itself is a home-made effigy, made of old clothes stuffed with paper, straw and old rags. It has to be on display if the children are to collect any money. On the evening of Guy Fawkes Day the Guy is burned on top of a bonfire, while fireworks are let off.

ll. 1–4: the reference to 'the hollow . . . stuffed men' combines allusions to Guy Fawkes, to *Julius Caesar* and to 'Heart of Darkness'. The first two sources are explained in the notes on pages 97–101. In 'Heart of Darkness', Marlow sees himself as a 'pretence' and sees other people in similar terms: one man a 'papier-maché Mephistopheles', another a 'harlequin', another 'in motley, as though he had absconded from a troupe of mimes. . . . His very existence was improbable, inexplicable'; and Kurtz, the central figure, is seen as a 'hollow sham'.
l. 6: 'whispers' are an instrument of fate in 'Heart of Darkness': it was the wilderness, the jungle that Kurtz exploited, as a trader, that 'had whispered to him tidings about himself he did not know . . . and the whisper proved irresistibly fascinat-ing. It echoed loudly within him because he was hollow at the core'. And the whisper of Kurtz's last words sounds a year after his death, when Marlow is begged to repeat them by Kurtz's fiancée.
ll. 11–12: this condition of unfulfilment is matched in the spiritual state of the shades described in the *Inferno* iii (see above, page 99) and in 'Heart of Darkness' by the members of the Eldorado Exploring Expedition: 'Their talk was . . . the talk of sordid buccaneers: it was reckless without hardihood, greedy without audacity, and cruel without courage . . . To tear treasure out of the bowels of the land was their desire, with no more moral purpose at the back of it than there is in burglars breaking into a safe.'

A second passage in 'Heart of Darkness' seems also to have been in Eliot's mind, Marlow's account of his fight against death: 'It is the most unexciting contest you can imagine. It takes place in an impalpable greyness, with nothing underfoot, with nothing around, without spectators, without clamour, without glory . . . in a sickly atmosphere of tepid scepticism, without much belief in your own right, and still less in that of your adversary . . . a vision of greyness without form', from which he emerges to find life 'like a passage through some inconceivable world that had no hope in it and no desire'. This experience is also relevant to lines 72–90.

ll. 13–15: the hollow men are reflecting on those who have passed from their world (or moral and spiritual state), 'death's dream kingdom' to 'death's other kingdom', a higher world, for those who are capable of looking with 'direct eyes'.

In the last cantos of the *Purgatorio* we read how Dante crosses from the Purgatorial world, passing through the two rivers (referred to above, see page 100) to approach the higher world of Beatrice. Until he is freed from shame and sin, he is unable to meet her gaze. In 'Heart of Darkness', Kurtz passes from life to death with a fixed 'stare' (referred to above, see page 101).

ll. 19–22: the image of 'eyes' that cannot be faced is important both in Dante and Conrad.

In Dante, the significant eyes are those of Beatrice: Dante is shamed and reproved by them; they recall to him his love for Beatrice during her life on earth and his subsequent infidelity; their divine beauty has a piercing brightness; and at their meeting in the Earthly Paradise he is like a small child, unable to meet her gaze.

In 'Heart of Darkness', Marlow encounters the force of eyes and glances wherever he goes—reproachful, fearful, intense; and the glance of Kurtz's fiancée, 'guileless, profound, confident, and trustful', yet, ironically, in all its qualities, dangerous, as it drives him into a 'hollowness' (see note to lines 37–38).

l. 19: Beatrice tells Dante how she came to him in his dreams to call him back to the path of virtue.

ll. 20–2: these lines can be interpreted as meaning that the eyes of line 19 are not encountered in 'death's dream kingdom'; in that kingdom, instead of eyes one sees the images of lines 23 to 28.

ll. 23-8: this seems to be a vision of 'death's other kingdom', glimpsed from afar and brokenly. The details seem to originate in *Purgatorio* xxviii-xxix, in the description of the Earthly Paradise: the birds and the breeze are singing in the trees, there is the sound of chanting and a light glows under the boughs. The star, here a 'fading star', is used by Dante as an image of God or of Mary.

ll. 31-2: the notion of 'deliberate disguises' is important in 'Heart of Darkness' (see note to lines 1-4).

ll. 33-4: these lines refer to the scarecrow and the country custom of hanging up the bodies of vermin or birds that damage the crops in order to scare off any others of the same species.

l. 35: In the *Inferno* the spirits are blown by the wind. In 'Heart of Darkness' there is a similar image in Marlow's account of a native who was killed only because he left open a shutter that should have been kept closed: 'He had no restraint, no restraint—just like Kurtz—a tree swayed by the wind.'

ll. 37-8: there is such a feared meeting in both Dante and Conrad. In *Purgatorio* xxx, Dante at last meets Beatrice. It is a fearful meeting for him, since it faces him with a divine beauty which reminds him of all his sins and failings. The River Lethe, which he has to cross to meet her, flows in 'everlasting shadow' (xxviii, 31-3).

In 'Heart of Darkness', there is the meeting between Marlow and Kurtz's fiancée, when he hands her the letters and picture left by the dead man. It is literally a 'twilight' meeting (see the quotation in the note to lines 61-2). Dusk is falling. This symbolizes Marlow's moral twilight. He had intended to tell her the bitter truth about Kurtz's life and death. But under the compulsion of her utter trust in Kurtz's goodness, he covers up, and falsifies the man's last words, reporting that he died with her name on his lips. This white lie is Marlow's own shameful submission to the 'heart of darkness', a darkness, so Conrad's story declares, whose twilight shadow is cast across the world.

ll. 39-44: These lines probably belong to the material discarded from *The Waste Land.* The 'stone images' and the 'broken stone' (line 50) are connected with idolatrous worship (see *The Waste Land*, note to line 22).

l. 47: cf. Marlow's words, 'We live, as we dream—alone.'

ll. 49-51: In 'Heart of Darkness' this corresponds to the pathetic trust that Kurtz's fiancée has in his nobility, his truth, his love for her. In point of fact, Kurtz sank from faithfulness to her to the worship of pagan forces.

ll. 52-6: the hollow valley is a province of 'death's dream kingdom'. In 'Heart of Darkness' it is the excavated valley, full of derelict objects and hopeless native labourers, that Marlow comes to on his way to the interior of the Congo: 'it seemed to me I had stepped into the gloomy circle of some Inferno. . . . Black shapes crouched, lay, sat between the trees, leaning against the trunks, clinging to the earth, half coming out, half effaced within the dim light, in all the attitudes of pain, abandonment, and despair.'

l. 56: Eliot may be playing upon the contrast with the whole and highly effective 'new jaw bone of an ass' (Judges xv, 15-19) with which Samson slew a thousand Philistines.

ll. 57-60: the association of these lines with Dante, and with the conspiracy situation in the Gunpowder Plot and *Julius Caesar*, is discussed on pages 97-9. The motif of conspiracy and plotting is also dominant in 'Heart of Darkness'. At the head office of the trading company on whose behalf he travels to the Congo, Marlow promised not to disclose any trade secrets: 'It was just as though I had been let into some conspiracy.' Later, at one of the trading stations, he finds the twenty or so white employees passing the time 'by backbiting and intriguing against each other in a foolish kind of way. There was an air of plotting about that station, but nothing came of it, of course. It was as unreal as everything else. . . .' And Kurtz is described as a man who 'would have been a splendid leader of an extreme party'.

l. 60 tumid river: in Dante, this corresponds with the River Acheron flowing around Hell. In 'Heart of Darkness', Marlow recollects the river up which he sailed to the 'heart of darkness' in the Congo as 'the infernal stream, the stream of darkness'.

ll. 61–2: in Dante, the reappearance of the eyes signifies Dante's meeting with Beatrice, a moment of 'hope' (line 66). In 'Heart of Darkness', Marlow's meeting with Kurtz's fiancée is invested by Conrad with a tone and feeling which is momentous and spiritually significant, with a similar emphasis upon a woman's eyes: 'The room seemed to have grown darker, as if all the sad light of the cloudy evening had taken refuge on her forehead. This fair hair, this pale visage, this pure brow, seemed surrounded by an ashy halo from which the dark eyes looked out at me. Their glance was guileless, profound, confident, and trustful.'

ll. 63–4: in the *Paradiso* the 'single star' is Dante's vision of the Virgin Mary (xxiii) and the 'rose' is his vision of Mary and the saints in heaven (xxxii).

l. 65: the significance of 'death's twilight kingdom', as a condition of spiritual power, seems to be brought out in the passage from Conrad just quoted; although we should not ignore the bitter irony: the purity and strength of the fiancée's virtue is the very thing that drives Marlow to his own 'hollowness' in lying to her.

ll. 68–71: a parody of the children's song-game, 'Here we go round the mulberry bush on a cold and frosty morning.'

ll. 72–90: cf.

> Between the acting of a dreadful thing
> And the first motion, all the interim is
> Like a phantasma, or a hideous dream:
> The genius and the mortal instruments
> Are then in council; and the state of man,
> Like to a little kingdom, suffers then
> The nature of an insurrection.

(*Julius Caesar* II, i, see note ii, page 98–9).

l. 76: Eliot accepted the suggestion, made in 1935, that this line was derived by him from 'Non sum qualis eram' ('I am not now as once I was'), the best-known poem by Ernest Dowson (1867–1900), in which the phrase 'There falls thy shadow' (and variants) is repeated. Eliot commented that 'This derivation had not occurred to my mind, but I believe it to be correct because the lines . . . have always run in my head'. Shadows, literal and figurative, always symbolic, are cast throughout the 'Heart of Darkness'. The boat on which Marlow travels upstream to Kurtz moves in shadows, once into a fog, through which is heard a cry 'as of infinite desolation' which turns into a shrieking but whose source and meaning they never know; men die with shadows across their faces; 'pain' is a shadow, feeding on Kurtz like a beast 'satiated and calm'; Marlow's knowledge of Kurtz's involvement with savage rites and ceremonies is a 'nightmare' secret, a 'shadow' which he keeps to himself, to deal with alone; Kurtz himself, drawn to these rites, appears to Marlow as a 'Shadow—that wandering and tormented thing'; and at the very end of the story, after Marlow's tale is finished, as the unnamed narrator describes the scene before him, we see that it is a shadow over all mankind: 'the tranquil waterway leading to the uttermost ends of the earth flowed sombre under an overcast sky—seemed to lead into the heart of an immense darkness'.

l. 77: 'For thine is the kingdom, the power, and the glory', from the Lord's Prayer, words which originally occur in 1 Chronicles xxix, 11, and in 15 there is a reference to the 'shadow': 'our days on the earth are as a shadow'.

l. 83: The fact that Eliot italicized these words suggests that we are to regard them as a quotation; they occur in *An Outcast of the Islands* (1896) by Joseph Conrad.

ll. 88–9: in Platonic philosophy, the essence is the inapprehensible ideal, which finds material expression in its descent to the lower, material plane of reality.

ll. 95–8: a parody, combining a line from the children's song 'Here we go round the mulberry bush'—'This is the way we clap our hands'—with the phrase 'world without end' from the prayer: 'Glory be to the Father, and to the Son, and to the

Holy Ghost, as it was in the beginning, is now, and ever shall be, world without end. Amen.'

l. 98 whimper: Eliot may have had in mind two lines from the poem 'Danny Deever' (1892) by Rudyard Kipling. Deever, a British soldier, is executed in front of his regiment for killing another comrade:

'What's that that whimpers over'ead?' said Files-on-Parade,
'It's Danny's soul that's passin' now,' the Colour-Sergeant said.

Eliot referred to this 'remarkable' poem in his Introduction to *A Choice of Kipling's Verse* (1941), quoting these lines and commenting that Kipling's choice of the word 'whimpers' is 'exactly right'.

The 'whimper' may also combine an allusive reference to Dante, suggesting the cry of a baby, the new-born leaving one world to enter another, just as at the end of the *Purgatorio* Dante is leaving the sinful, fallen world in the presence of Beatrice in the Earthly Paradise. In xxx, 43 ff. and xxxi, 64 ff., he stands before her, shamed and conscience-stricken, repentant and silent, like a child before a stern mother.

ASH-WEDNESDAY

ASH-WEDNESDAY

For details of composition and publication (1930) see Appendix

Prefatory Note: readers may find it helpful to refer to the Appendix which gives details of the indicative titles which Eliot originally provided for the sections of the poem.

Title: in the Christian calendar this is the first day of Lent, a period of forty days penance and fasting to commemorate the forty days Christ spent fasting in the wilderness, where he was tempted by Satan and triumphed over him (see Matthew iv, 1–11; Luke iv, 1–13). It is a period when the Christian repents for his past sins and turns away from the world towards God.

In the Church ceremony for Ash Wednesday, the priest marks the foreheads of the laity with ashes in the form of a cross, saying these words: 'Remember, O man, that thou art dust, and unto dust thou shalt return', a version of God's words to Adam (Genesis iii, 19).

I

l. 1: a translation of 'Perch 'io non spero di tornar giammai', the opening line of 'Ballata, written in exile at Saranza' by Guido Cavalcanti (1255–1300). The poet is heart-broken and exiled, expecting never again to see his lady and thinking of death. And besides this theme of worldly loss and resignation, there is also the spiritual act of turning to God, seen in its penitential aspect, as in Joel ii, 12: '. . . turn ye even to me with all your heart, and with fasting, and with weeping, and with mourning.'

l. 4: a version of a line from Shakespeare's Sonnet xxix, 'Desiring this man's art and that man's scope.' The poet describes his troubled state of mind when he is alone and outcast, a bitter, discontented sadness which is transformed to joy at the thought of his beloved.

l. 6 agéd eagle: in mediaeval Christian allegory the eagle, in its old age, is able to renew its youth in the light of the sun and in the waters of a fountain; this signifies an access of spiritual life through a turning to God and through baptism.

l. 10 infirm glory: Eliot may have picked up this striking phrase from *Night and Day* (1919), a novel by Virginia Woolf, where it refers, half ironically, to the state of those, now elderly, who were once famous: 'all the poets, all the novelists, all the beautiful women and distinguished men'.

l. 33: Eliot seems to be touching on the Biblical story of the eviction from the Garden of Eden and the original sin then laid on mankind for the 'transgression' of Adam and Eve (see Genesis iii).

ll. 40-1: the close of the Roman Catholic prayer, the Hail Mary, asking the Blessed Virgin Mary to intercede and give spiritual aid on behalf of sinful mankind.

II

l. 42 juniper-tree: cf. the Biblical story of Elijah. Jezebel threatened him with death. He went into the wilderness and under the shade of a juniper-tree prayed that God would take his life. Instead, God sent him food (see I Kings xix, 1-8).

leopards: leopards are named as God's agents of destruction in Jeremiah v, 6 and Hosea xiii, 7. The entire line is much speculated about. When, in 1929, Eliot was asked what it meant, he simply answered 'I mean' and then recited the line without comment.

ll. 43–7: cf. the vision of Ezekiel, in which God predicts the spiritual regeneration of the Israelites, his chosen people: 'And he said unto me, Son of man, can these bones live . . . he said unto me, Prophesy upon these bones and say unto them, O ye dry bones hear the voice of the Lord' (see Ezekiel xxxvii, 1–10).

ll. 62–4: when he was ignored by the people, the prophet Jeremiah addressed the Earth; now the prophet has only the wind to hear him.

l. 65 the burden of the grasshopper: This is a punning reference to Ecclesiastes xii, 5: 'the grasshopper shall be a burden' (a plague). Eliot is playing with another meaning, 'burden' as a song.

ll. 66–88: these lines imitate the Roman Catholic Litany to the Blessed Virgin Mary, a form of solemn public supplication.

l. 69 Rose: Mary is referred to as a rose in the Litany.

ll. 93–5: cf. 'This is the land which ye shall divide by lot unto the tribes of Israel for inheritance, and these are their portions, saith the Lord God' (Ezekiel xlviii, 29), God's instructions to the prophet in his vision. In xxxvii, 15–22 God instructs Ezekiel to unite the divided tribes of Joseph and Judah.

III

ll. 100–101: cf. 'the demon of doubt which is inseparable from the spirit of belief', Eliot's description of the demon faced by the French philosopher Blaise Pascal (1623–62), see Eliot's Introduction to *Pascal's Pensées* (1931).

ll. 117–19: these fragments are taken from Matthew viii, 8: 'Lord, I am not worthy that thou shouldst come under my roof: but speak the word only, and my servant shall be healed.' These are the words of the centurion at Capernaum, one of whose servants was ill. He asked Christ to cure him, crediting him with the power to do this at a distance, without needing to visit the sick man at his house. Christ pointed to the Centurion's trust in him as a supreme example of faith.

The first part of the sentence is spoken by the priest, as an act of humility, just before he takes the sacrament.

IV

In this section Eliot makes extensive general reference to the final cantos of the *Purgatorio*, where Dante reaches the summit of the Mount of Purgatory, enters the Earthly Paradise and sees Beatrice, his beloved on earth, now a figure of divine beauty, reminding him of his sinful past. This source is described more fully in the notes to 'The Hollow Men', see especially pages 99–100.

l. 120 violet: the liturgical colour for penitence and intercession.

l. 123: the liturgical colours of the Blessed Virgin Mary.

ll. 127–8: These lines echo a line from Baudelaire: 'Makes the rocks pour forth water and the desert flourish', an echo which is more evident in the phrasing and rhythm of the original French: 'Fait couler le rocher et fleurir le désert' (from 'Bohémiens en Voyage'). In this poem, 'The Travelling Gipsies', it is the goddess Cybele who eases the journey of the gipsy band.

l. 130: be mindful. From the words of Arnaut Daniel to Dante, praying him to remember, when he returns to Earth, Daniel's suffering for his lust (see page 92, note to line 427 of *The Waste Land*).

ll. 137–8 Redeem/The time: Eliot is using a phrase usually associated with the wise and proper use of one's life for Christian purposes, as St. Paul employed it in his Epistles: 'Walk in wisdom toward them that are without, redeeming the time' (Colossians iv, 5); 'See then that ye walk circumspectly, not as fools, but as wise, Redeeming the time, because the days are evil' (Ephesians v, 15). In both these Epistles, St. Paul is advising early Christian communities on their duty towards God and men.

The modern significance of this phrase for Eliot can be seen in his essay 'Thoughts after Lambeth' (1931): 'redeeming the time: so that the Faith may be preserved alive through the dark ages before us; to renew and rebuild civilization, and save the World from suicide'.

ll. 139–40: In *Purgatorio* xxix, Dante sees the Divine Pageant, in which Beatrice is drawn by a griffon in a triumphal chariot. Eliot associates the 'pageantry' of that scene with 'the world of what I call the *high dream*, and the modern world seems capable only of the *low dream*' ('Dante').

l. 141 veiled: Beatrice is veiled before Dante is permitted to see the divine beauty of her face (*Purgatorio* xxx,31); also see lines 168, 172, 177 below).

ll. 142–3: Priapus, a Greek god of fertility, was usually honoured with statues in gardens and orchards, although the reference to the 'flute' would suggest Pan with his pipes, the Greek god of shepherds and huntsmen.

ll. 144, 147: Dante draws attention to the singing of the birds and to the song of the wind in the trees as he enters the Garden of Eden, *Purgatorio* xxviii.

l. 146: Eliot's phrasing 'the word unheard, unspoken', developed in lines 149–54, suggests that he has in mind John i, 1 and the image developed by Lancelot Andrewes, see page 44, note to lines 18–19 of 'Gerontion'.

l. 148: this is a phrase from a Roman Catholic prayer addressed to the Blessed Virgin Mary, usually said at the end of the mass, and concluding 'and after this our exile show unto us the blessed fruit of thy womb, Jesus'.

V

ll. 156–7: The 'world-whirled' homophone is probably copied from the pun-etymology of stanza 34 of *Orchestra* by Sir John Davies (1565–1618): 'Behold the world, how it is whirled round!/And for it is so whirled, is named so.'

l. 158: from Micah vi, 3. The Lord cries to the people, reproaching them for their departure from the ways of virtue and faith. These words have been taken into the liturgy of the Church. In the Roman Catholic mass for Good Friday, the day of the crucifixion, these words are part of the Reproaches, a liturgy in which Christ on the cross speaks to the people: 'O my people, what have I done unto thee? Or in what have I grieved thee? Because I brought thee out of the land of Egypt, thou hast prepared a cross for thy Saviour.'

l. 167: as Dante, ashamed for his sins, is unable to face Beatrice.

VI

l. 191 (Bless me father): 'Bless me, father, for I have sinned' are the opening words of the penitent to the priest in the Roman Catholic form of confession.

l. 202: false and delusive dreams pass out of the ivory gate of the underworld on their way to earth (see Virgil, *Aeneid* vi).

l. 214: the words of Piccarda (see page 57, note to line 24 of 'The Cooking Egg') to Dante, *Paradiso* iii, 85–7: 'Our peace is His will, His will is our peace. It is that sea towards which moves all that it creates and all that nature makes.'

ll. 216–17: in one of the forms of the Roman Catholic litany Mary is addressed as 'Stella Maris' ('Star of the Sea').

l. 218: 'Suffer me not to be separated from thee' is a line from the Roman Catholic hymn 'Soul of Christ'.

l. 219: in the Roman Catholic mass, this is the response to the words of the priest, 'Hear my prayer, O Lord'. The sentence as a whole comes from Psalms cii, 1.

ARIEL POEMS

ARTHUR POLME

JOURNEY OF THE MAGI

Published 1927

The Magi: the three wise men who came from the east to honour the new-born Jesus. Their story is told in Matthew ii, 1–12. Later tradition identified them as three Kings—Balthazar (King of Chaldea), Gaspar (the Ethiopian King of Tarshish) and Melchior (King of Nubia).

In the final section of the poem Eliot seems to be exploiting the associations of the word magi with the priestly class of magicians in Ancient Persia.

ll. 1–5: adapted from a nativity sermon preached before James I by Lancelot Andrewes on Christmas Day 1622: 'A cold coming they had of it at this time of year, just the worst time of year to take a journey, and specially a long journey in. The ways deep, the weather sharp, the days short, the sun furthest off, *in solstitio brumali*, "the very dead of winter".' Immediately before this passage, Andrewes reviews the hardships of the journey, details of which Eliot uses in lines 6–20.

ll. 21–8: Eliot has explained that certain images are charged for him with a personal yet inexplicable meaning, representing 'the depths of feeling into which we cannot peer'; and amongst his examples he mentions 'six ruffians seen through an open window playing cards at night at a small French railway junction where there was a water-mill . . .' (*The Use of Poetry and the Use of Criticism*, 1935).

l. 24: there were three crosses on Calvary, those of Christ and the two 'malefactors' (see Luke xxiii, 32–3).

l. 25 white horse: in Revelation vi, 2 and xix, 11–14, Christ the conqueror rides on a white horse.

l. 27: a glancing allusion to the Biblical accounts of the betrayal of Christ for 30 pieces of silver and the soldiers dicing for the robes of Christ at the crucifixion (see, for example, Matthew xxvi, 14–15; xxvii, 35).

ll. 32 to end: the tone of mystified acceptance in which the magus speaks may have been suggested to Eliot by a passage in Andrewes' sermon where the rhetorical question is posed—what did the magi find?: 'No sight to comfort them, nor a word for which they any whit the wiser; nothing worth their travel. . . . Well, they will take Him as they find Him, and all this notwithstanding, worship Him for all that.'

ll. 33–5: these lines set the dramatic situation. The magus is reminiscing for the benefit of a listener who is to make a record of these events and experiences. Eliot may have taken the idea for this situation from 'The Adoration of the Magi', a prose piece by the Irish poet, W. B. Yeats (1865–1939), then recently re-published in a volume which Yeats entitled *Mythologies* (1925). Yeats tells how three old men sat by his fireside and told their story. They insisted that he 'take notes' so that he 'might have the exact words'.

Further, the very specific details and the broken utterances of Eliot's magus may be stylistic devices suggested by Yeats's account: 'Now one talked and now another, and they often interrupted one another, with a desire like that of countrymen, when they tell a story, to leave no detail untold' (p. 308).

l. 41 the old dispensation: the 'new' dispensation is the reign of Christianity; see Paul's address to the early Christians, in which he speaks of 'the dispensation of the Grace of God' and his 'knowledge in the mystery of Christ' (Ephesians iii, 2–4).

A SONG FOR SIMEON

Published 1928

Simeon: the story of Simeon is told in Luke ii, 25–35. He is an old and devout Jew, living in Jerusalem, awaiting the coming of the Messiah. The Holy Ghost reveals to him that he is not to die until he has seen Christ, and guides him to the temple, where the new-born Jesus has been brought by Joseph and Mary for the circumcision. Simeon takes Jesus in his arms, his destiny now fulfilled: 'Lord, now lettest thou thy servant depart in peace, according to thy word: For mine eyes have seen thy salvation, Which thou hast prepared before the face of all people. . . .'

Simeon also prophesies to Mary the suffering to come: 'Behold this child is set for the fall and rising again of many in Israel, and for a sign which shall be spoken against; (Yea, a sword shall pierce through thy own soul also), that the thoughts of many hearts may be revealed.' These words look forward darkly to the sufferings of Christ and the persecution of the early Christians, to which Eliot refers in line 13 onwards.

l. 1 Roman hyacinths: Roman, because Judaea was then under Roman rule; 'blooming in bowls', because the Roman variety is a special type of flower suitable for forced indoor cultivation.
l. 8: a liturgical form of appeal for God's blessing.
l. 14: see second note below to line 19.
l. 17 scourges: Christ was later scourged at the order of Pilate, the Roman Governor.
   lamentation: Luke xxxiii, 27–9 tells of the crowd of women, bewailing and lamenting, that followed Christ out of Jerusalem on the way to the crucifixion.

l. 19 stations: the Stations of the Cross is a Roman Catholic devotion conducted before a series of fourteen images or pictures representing the events from the time that Christ was sentenced to death, to the placing of his corpse in the sepulchre.

the mountain of desolation: Calvary, where the crucifixion took place. Eliot seems to have made up this phrase from Mark xiii, 14, in a passage where Christ is forewarning the disciples of the persecution yet to be faced: 'But when ye shall see the abomination of desolation . . . then let them that be in Judaea flee to the mountains.'

l. 20: the Gospels record that Christ died at 'the ninth hour'.

l. 22: Eliot's association of the 'Infant' and the 'unspeaking and unspoken Word' suggests that he has in mind John i, 1 and the image developed by Lancelot Andrewes, see page 44, note to lines 18–19 of 'Gerontion'.

l. 23 Israel's: Israel was the community promised by God to the Israelites, his chosen people, where they could live in freedom after their years of wandering and captivity.

ll. 27–8: a version of Simeon's prophetic warning to Mary (see head-note on Simeon); he is referring to the suffering Mary will have to endure at the sight of her son's torment and death.

ll. 32–3: an adaptation of Simeon's words (see head-note on Simeon).

ANIMULA

Published 1929

Title: Latin, meaning a little soul. Eliot seems to have in mind the most notable use of the word, in the poem addressed by the Roman Emperor Hadrian (76–138 A.D.) to his soul, with the first line 'Animula uagula blandula' ('Little soul—fleeting away and charming').

l. 1: this line Eliot has derived from a passage in Dante, *Purgatorio* xvi, 85–8, where the poet is discussing the nature of the human soul and its need for discipline: 'From the hands of Him who loves her before she is, there issues like a little child that plays, with weeping and laughing, the simple soul, that knows nothing except that, coming from the hands of a glad creator, she turns willingly to everything that delights her. First she tastes the flavour of a trifling good; then, is beguiled, and pursues it, if neither guide nor check withhold her. Therefore laws were needed as a curb; a ruler was needed, who should at least see afar the tower of the true City.' (The translation is that given by Eliot in 'Dante').

l. 19 'is and seems': A concept taken from the philosopher F. H. Bradley (see *The Waste Land*, note to line 411): the distinction is between appearance ('seems') and reality ('is'). In itself reality is an awareness to the gap between the actual and the ideal, giving rise to the notions of obligation, duty, and ethical value contained in the philosophical term 'imperatives', those considerations that move us to act morally.

l. 23 Encyclopaedia Britannica: the 'British Encyclopaedia', the largest and, by tradition, the most authoritative encyclopaedia in English.

l. 31 viaticum: the last sacrament of communion given to the dying.

ll. 32–3 Guiterriez, Boudin: in answer to a researcher's inquiry Eliot said that these two men 'represent different types of career, the successful person of the machine age and someone who was killed in the last war' (meaning the 1914–18 war).

l. 36 Floret: Eliot also commented on this name, saying that the figure is 'entirely imaginary' and that 'no identification' is to be made. But he added that the name Floret 'might suggest not wholly irrelevantly to some minds certain folklore memories'. This rather cryptic remark may be Eliot's way of saying that some readers might be reminded of two figures of Greek legend, Actaeon the hunter, who was torn to death by his own hands, or of Adonis, the beautiful youth who was killed by a wild boar, as was the god Attis in the ancient vegetation cults.

l. 37: in the Roman Catholic prayer, the 'Hail Mary', the last word of this line is 'death'.

MARINA

Published 1930

Marina: the daughter of Pericles in *Pericles, Prince of Tyre* by Shakespeare. Her name is associated with the sea (Latin *mare*, adjective *marinus, marina*). In the play, we hear how she was born at sea, as a baby lost to her father, believed by him to be dead, and is in womanhood restored to him seemingly miraculously. Eliot considered this to be one of the great moments in literature, as we learn from his remarks in a lecture given in 1937: 'To my mind the finest of all the "recognition scenes" is Act v, i of that very great play *Pericles*. It is a perfect example of the "ultra-dramatic", a dramatic action of beings who are more than human, or rather, seen in a light more than that of day.'

Epigraph: 'What is this place, what country, what region of the world?' These are the words of Hercules as he returns to sanity, having in madness killed his wife and children; from the play *Hercules Furens* (line 1138) by Seneca (died A.D. 65).

In 1930 Eliot wrote that he had used these two dramatic references to effect a 'criss cross'. Their contrast is clear. *Pericles* is concerned with truth and revelation as miraculously wonderful experiences. But in *Hercules Furens* the hero, Hercules, has been driven mad as a punishment for his pride. He emerges from insanity to a discovery of horror.

l. 6 dog: for the dog as an image of menace and evil, see note to *The Waste Land*, line 74.
ll. 17–18: cf. 'But are you flesh and blood?/Have you a working pulse?' (*Pericles* v, i), the wondering questions of Pericles

as it begins to dawn upon him that Marina may, by some miracle, be his daughter, alive. Eliot seems to be combining this allusion with verbal echoes of the scene in Shakespeare's *Macbeth* (I, iii): on the Heath the first Witch greets Banquo as 'Lesser than Macbeth, and greater'; and the Second Witch, 'Not so happy, yet much Happier.' Banquo, like Eliot's Pericles, questions the nature of what he sees.

l. 28 garboard strake: a single breadth of planking next to the keel.

CHORUSES FROM 'THE ROCK'

CHORUSES FROM 'THE ROCK'

Published 1934

The Rock is a verse pageant-play, accompanied by music and ballet, which was written in support of a fund to preserve the old churches of London and for church-building in new housing areas. Eliot provided the verse choruses, and some of the prose dialogue for a prepared scenario, telling of the development of the Christian church, linking this to work on an actual church building in contemporary London in 1934.

Much of the verse is deeply grounded in the Bible—in its language, imagery and rhythms—and the notes attend only to specific references. The second area of reference is to life in contemporary London, and explanatory notes are provided.

Title: Eliot is drawing upon the Biblical use of the word 'rock', signifying God in his aspect of supporting strength for weak mankind, as in Psalms lxxxix, 26: 'Thou art my father, my God, and the rock of my salvation', and in Matthew xvi, 18, the words of Christ to Peter: 'thou art Peter, and upon this rock I will build my church.'

I

ll. 1, 2: constellations of stars.
l. 11 Word: cf. 'In the beginning was the Word, and the Word was with God, and the Word was God' (John i, 1).
l. 18 Dust: cf. the words of God to Satan in the Garden of Eden: 'upon thy belly shalt thou go, and dust shalt thou eat all the days of thy life'; and God's words to Adam, 'for dust thou art, and unto dust shalt thou return' (Genesis iii, 14, 19).

l. 19 the timekept City: the business area of London, governed by time, as the office workers come in the morning and leave at night and as the clocks of the many city churches sound the hours (aspects of the city which enter *The Waste Land* at lines 61–8).

l. 20: Eliot plays upon two meanings: foreign merchant ships on the River Thames; the flow of money in and out of the city, then the world's great financial centre, for the support of business overseas.

l. 22 chop-houses: the traditional city restaurants, serving good quick lunches for businessmen.

l. 29: Hindhead in Surrey is a beauty-spot within easy motoring-distance of London, as is Maidenhead, a small town beside the Thames west of London.

l. 49: to tread the grapes, the ancient method of getting juice for wine, is a Biblical metaphor for doing the work of the Lord, often the work of the God of wrath, as in Isaiah lxiii, 3: 'I have trodden the winepress alone; and of the people there was none with me; for I will tread them in my anger, and trample them in my fury.'

l. 57: an echo of many Biblical injunctions to serve God willingly, to become perfect in one's determination to serve God.

ll. 58–9: the Biblical metaphor instructs man to live a Christian life without regard to its rewards or punishments.

l. 72 tube-train: a train on London's underground railway, trains which are frequently packed tight with passengers.

ll. 102, 105 In this land: With this phrase God promises to the prophet Jeremiah a place where the faithful will prosper (Jeremiah xxxii, 41, 43). Eliot parodies both the Biblical sentiments and the cadence of their statement.

l. 108 'The Times': then England's most formally respectable daily newspaper, whose obituaries of the great are still world-renowned.

II

v. 3 cornerstone: an image found in Psalms cxviii, 22 and repeated in the Gospels.

v. 7 the Spirit . . . on the face of the waters: 'And the Spirit of God moved upon the face of the waters' (Genesis i, 1) as he prepared to create light in the darkness and void before the creation of the world. The comparison, which follows, with the tortoise, may refer to a Hindu creation myth, in which the world itself is on the tortoise's back.

v. 8 love our neighbour: one of the tenets of Christianity, as in, 'Thou shalt love thy neighbour as thyself' (Matthew xix, 19).

l. 16 Whipsnade: a zoo near London.

v. 37 Temple: used in the Bible to signify the Church of God.

l. 44 ribbon roads: roads so-called because of the ribbon-like lines of houses built on either side, a phenomenon of the 1920's and 30's, especially around London.

III

ll. 1–19: the style of this section echoes the way in which the Old Testament prophets record the words of God, coming to them in dreams and visions.

l. 15 race reports: newspaper reports of horse and greyhound races provided for gamblers.

l. 20 East: the East End of London, a dockland area then filled with slums.

l. 31–6: Eliot is characterizing the prosperous middle-class suburbs of London, the flower-gardens and the tennis-courts.

l. 41: cavies, guinea pigs; *marmots,* rodents of the squirrel family.

l. 65: Eliot is playing upon the association of the stars with human fortune in astrology, the ancient art of prophecy; but today men seek another, financial fortune on the stock-exchange, in ordinary (Eliot's 'common') or preference shares.

VII

The structure of this section is derived from the Biblical account of the creation in Genesis.

v. 1: cf. 'In the beginning God created the heaven and the earth. And the earth was without form, and void; and darkness was upon the face of the deep' (Genesis i, 1–2).

v. 7: cf. 'And the spirit of God moved upon the face of the waters' (Genesis i, 2).

v. 10 Good and Evil: this was the knowledge with which Satan tempted Eve, to be gained by eating of the fruit from 'the tree of knowledge of good and evil' which God had forbidden Adam to eat from, under pain of death (see Genesis ii–iii).

v. 18 moment: the birth of Christ.

v. 22 Passion: the period of the crucifixion is known as Passion Week, from the agony in the garden, the arrest, the trial and scourging, to the resurrection.

Sacrifice: the death of Christ seen as God's sacrifice of his only son on behalf of mankind.

v. 29 Dialectic: uncapitalized, dialectic is the investigation of truth by critical rational discussion; capitalized, it probably refers to the worship of an ideology, most likely Marxist Socialism.

IX

ll. 1–15: as in Section III, lines 1–18, Eliot is echoing the form of address employed by God in speaking to his prophets.

l. 15 communion of saints: a phrase from the *Credo* (*I believe*) where the Christian declares his trust in the tenets of his faith.

l. 25: a version of the traditional grace spoken before meals: 'Bless, O Lord, this food (*or* these gifts) to our use and us to thy service; for Jesus Christ's sake, Amen.'

l. 44 cf. 'O World invisible, we view thee', the opening line to 'The Kingdom of God', a devotional poem by Francis Thompson (1859–1907).

X

v. 7 the great snake: the Devil, combining his Biblical character of snake (see Genesis iii) and sea-monster (Job xli, 1).

l. 17: see note to IX, line 44.

APPENDIX

The Composition of *The Waste Land,* *The Hollow Men* and *Ash-Wednesday*

To understand these three longer works we need, in each case, to have a proper sense of the poem's total structure and internal development; we need to be able to follow the poem's meaning, as it grows from section to section. An interpretational problem, and thus not touched upon in the detailed notes to the poems, is that the connections between the separate sections are not always easy to grasp—they are associational and thematic links, which the reader must discover for himself, just as he must judge for himself the degree of unity attained within each of the three poems. As an item of background information, it may be useful to know something of the writing and publishing history of these poems, for there is one significant fact, common to all three: each of these works was built up gradually from poems or fragments of verse that Eliot had already previously published or had kept by him for several years (as, too, had 'Prufrock' grown, as Eliot said, out of 'several fragments'); and it was not until relatively late that Eliot saw how these bits and pieces fitted together to form the longer single works. This we can see indirectly in the bibliographical details set out below.

The earliest of the three poems was *The Waste Land,* published in October 1922, and written or assembled during the previous twenty months. Eliot sent Ezra Pound a manuscript towards the end of 1921. It was then (in Eliot's words) a 'sprawling, chaotic poem'; it left Pound's hands 'reduced to about half its size'. Pound suggested that material should be pruned; he indicated detailed verbal changes (fully visible on

the manuscript, of which a facsimile will be available in 1971);
and in all this it seems that Eliot followed his friend's advice.
More than that, Pound helped Eliot towards an understanding
of the poem's unity. Early in 1922 Eliot asked whether it might
not be advisable to omit Section IV. Pound's answer was firm,
and helpfully interpretative: 'I DO advise keeping Phlebas. In
fact I more'n advise. Phlebas is an integral part of the poem;
the card pack introduces him, the drowned phoen. sailor.
And he is needed ABsolootly where he is. Must stay in.' (The
bizarre spelling is Pound's own personal style of emphasis.)
In the event, Eliot retained Phlebas.

Eliot's uncertainty is worth remarking on, for Section IV of
The Waste Land was not, at the time, an original and new piece
of verse; it was an English version (with some changes) of the
last seven lines of 'Dans le Restaurant', a French poem he had
written in 1916 or 17. And this is not the only part of *The
Waste Land* to have been derived from earlier material. When
Eliot showed the published version to his friend and fellow-
poet Conrad Aiken, Aiken found himself reading a work some
of which was already known to him. This he recollected, years
later: '. . . I had long been familiar with such passages as, 'A
woman drew her long black hair out tight,' which I had seen
as poems, or part-poems in themselves. And now saw inserted
into *The Waste Land* as into a mosaic.' We can consider the
force of these remarks alongside Pound's comment, made in
March 1922, that *The Waste Land* was 'a series of poems'.

Our authority for the composite nature of the other two
poems is Eliot himself. *Ash-Wednesday* 'like "The Hollow Men",
[it] originated out of separate poems. . . . Then gradually I
came to see it as a sequence. That's one way in which my mind
does seem to have evolved through the years poetically—doing
things separately and then seeing the possibility of focusing
them together, altering them, and making a kind of whole of
them.' These remarks, given at an interview, accord with the
publishing history of 'The Hollow Men'. The poem, as we
know it today, was first published in 1925; but four of the five
sections had by then already appeared in print: Section I

APPENDIX

(dated November 1924) in the periodical *Commerce* (Winter 1924); Sections II and IV in a group entitled 'Three Poems' in *The Criterion*, January 1925; Section III as one of *Doris's Dream Songs*, 1924. A version of 'The Hollow Men' (Sections I, II, and IV), was published in *The Dial*, March 1925. Later in the year came the final version, incorporating the already published Section III and the hitherto unpublished Section V. The process of assembling this poem may have been difficult for Eliot, if, as it seems likely, the sections were developed from the materials left over from *The Waste Land*, the lines which Pound had advised Eliot to discard; other *Waste Land* materials were used in *Marina* and *The Dry Salvages* (and we might note that, according to Eliot, *Burnt Norton* 'began with bits cut out of *Murder in the Cathedral*').

The publishing history of *Ash-Wednesday* is similar. When the six sections were published together under the single title in 1930, three had been published before, as single, independent poems. Section II appeared in the *Saturday Review of Literature*, December 1927, under the title 'Salutation'; Section I in *Commerce*, Spring 1928, with the title 'Perch'io Non Spero'; and Section III in *Commerce*, Autumn 1929, entitled 'Som de L'Escalina'. Sections IV and V, previously unpublished, were then added to complete the sequence.

As a footnote, it may assist some readers to follow the system of titles which Eliot gave to the separate poems. 'Salutation' (Section II), in its ordinary sense, is an apt title; but beyond the word's normal meaning Eliot probably had in mind a specific Dantean salutation, that in *Vita Nuova* iii, where the poet is greeted by the Lady 'with a salutation of such virtue that I thought then to see the world of blessedness'. The title 'Perch'io Non Spero' (Section I) is the opening words to a poem by Cavalcanti; Eliot used these words for his own first line, 'Because I do not hope' (see page 111). 'Som de L'Escalina' (Section III) are the words addressed to Dante as he climbs the third section of stairway on the Mount of Purgatory, at the top of which—'the topmost of the stair'—is the Garden of Eden. The speaker is the Provençal poet Arnaut

APPENDIX

Daniel, consigned to Purgatory for lustfulness. The relevance of the Dante source (given in full on page 92, note to *The Waste Land*, line 427) is apparent in Eliot's references in this poem to the 'stair' and to sensual distractions, in lines 106–15.

The complete *Ash-Wednesday* was eventually published with the sections numbered, not titled. But up to the last moment Eliot had retained a system of titles. These were noted by his friend and publisher Leonard Woolf, who saw a typescript. Sections I and III carried the titles they bore as separate poems. Section II had a different title—'Jausen lo Jorn'—a phrase spoken by Arnaut Daniel in the same speech from which Eliot had taken the title for Section III; it is italicized here: 'And I see *with joy the day* for which I hope, before me.' This change of title suggests that Eliot wanted to draw attention to the purgatorial aspect of the section. Section IV was headed 'Vestita di Color di Fiamma' ('clad in the colour of flame'), a phrase which occurs in the description of Beatrice (*Purgatorio* xxx, 33) at the Divine Pageant. This helps to identify the spiritual nature of the Lady in Eliot's poem and suggests the basis for the details in line 140 (see note on page 115). Section V was entitled 'La Sua Volontade' ('His Will'), taken from the line 'la sua volontade è nostra pace' ('his will is our peace') (*Paradiso* iii, 85; see page 116, note to *Ash-Wednesday*, line 214).

Why Eliot decided to strip the poem of these titles is an open question. He may have felt that the specific reference of these quotation-titles was limiting, that the poem would be better understood without the Dantean reminders. Whatever the reason, Eliot removed these literary sign-posts.